ON TIPTOE WITH
JOY

To Jon & Jean
from Jaytie Seamands

ON TIPTOE WITH JOY

John T. Seamands

BAKER BOOK HOUSE

Grand Rapids, Michigan

ISBN: 0-8010-7989-6

Acknowledgement is made for permission to quote from copy-
righted versions of the Bible: *Revised Standard Version,* Copyright, 1946, 1952, Division of Christian Education, National
Council of the Churches of Christ in the United States of
America; *The Bible: A New Translation* by James Moffatt,
Copyright 1950, 1952, 1953, 1954 by James A. R. Moffatt,
published by Harper and Row; *The New Testament in Modern
English,* Copyright 1958, J. B. Phillips, used by permission of
the Macmillan Company.

Lovingly dedicated

to my father,

veteran missionary to India,

whose radiant joy has been

a splendid example of the

Spirit-filled life.

Foreword

Here is a spiritually helpful, intellectually challenging, and interesting book. It is an excellent volume for use in private or group meditations and Bible study. I recommend that it be studiously and prayerfully read by fathers, mothers, young people in high school and college, and by all others who wish to be at their best in relation to God and man.

The theme of this book is the Holy Spirit and the blessed life that He makes possible for those who respond to His leading.

The promise of "another Comforter" who would reprove, instruct, and empower the believer and glorify Christ was not given only for first-century Christians, but for all who in every century and in every age will tarry until He comes upon them. This Comforter, the Holy Spirit, is as necessary to us of today, wherever and in whatever condition we live, as He was to those who received Him in the first Pentecost.

The author, John T. Seamands; his father, E. A. Seamands, to whom this book is dedicated; and his younger brother, David A. Seamands, have served God with a devotion, persistence, and effectiveness that have made them recognized exemplars of the life to which this book calls so persuasively.

—J. WASKOM PICKETT
Bishop of the Methodist Church

Contents

Preface

Wherever the Holy Spirit dwells in His fulness there will be joy—abiding joy.

Joy is not one of the primary results of the fulness of the Holy Spirit, and therefore should not be sought for as an end in itself. The primary results are personal purity and power for effective service. Joy is one of the by-products of the indwelling Presence. But it is one of the chief by-products and certainly is the goal of all people. It is indeed the badge of the true disciple of Jesus Christ.

In the Scriptures joy is often linked with the ministry of the Holy Spirit. In the list of the fruit of the Spirit, the apostle Paul mentions joy immediately after the primary virtue, love (Gal. 5:22). In his Epistle to the Ephesians he connects melody and singing with the fulness of the Holy Spirit. "Be filled with the Spirit; speaking to yourselves in psalms and hymns and spiritual songs, singing and making melody in your heart to the Lord" (Eph. 5:18-19). To the church at Rome he writes: "The kingdom of God is not meat and drink; but righteousness, and peace, and joy in the Holy Ghost" (Rom. 14:17).

Joy was one of the chief characteristics of the early Christians, who were men and women filled with the Holy Spirit. Luke writes of the three thousand who were converted on the Day of Pentecost that "they, continuing daily with one accord in the temple, and breaking bread from house to house, did eat their meat with *gladness* and singleness of heart, praising God, and having favour with all the people" (Acts 2:46-47). When the apostles were put in prison and later threatened with further punishment if they continued to preach in the name of Jesus, "they departed from the presence of the council, *rejoicing* that they were counted worthy to suffer shame for his name" (Acts 5:41). When Philip went up to the city of Samaria and started a great revival among the people, "there was great joy in that city" (8:8). When the Ethiopian official was baptized by the evangelist Philip, he went on his way *rejoicing*" (8:39). When Paul and Barnabas were driven out of Antioch in Pisidia by the Jews and the new converts were also threatened, "the disciples were filled with *joy,* and with the Holy Ghost" (13:52). When Paul and Silas were beaten and cast into prison in Philippi, "at midnight . . . [they] sang praises unto God; and the prisoners heard them" (16:25).

It is quite evident that a great many Christians of our day do not experience "the joy of the Lord." Their lives are more like funeral dirges than symphonies of joy. Almost every Sunday of the year I am in a different church, preaching to a strange congregation. As I look out across the audience, I invariably notice that a good percentage of the members are not singing the hymns, and those who are actually singing don't seem to be enjoying themselves very much. No wonder Nieztsche, the German philosopher and agnostic, said that Christians would have to look more redeemed before he gave attention to their claims.

Could it be that we are lacking in joy because we are not experiencing the fulness of the Holy Spirit? *This I most sincerely believe.* We have not emphasized as we should the doctrine and experience of the Holy Spirit in our seminaries, our churches, our preaching, and teaching. In the average pulpit across the land the Holy Spirit is mentioned only when the Apostles' Creed is recited or the benediction is pronounced. The Church must make central in its teaching the person and ministry of the Holy Spirit.

This book on the Holy Spirit is a sincere attempt to reemphasize the doctrine of the Holy Spirit in relationship to everyday Christian living. When we recapture the fulness of the Holy Spirit, then we shall begin to experience the joy of the Lord in our hearts, reflect it on our faces, and demonstrate it in our lives. If through the reading of these messages even a small number of church members will become Spirit-filled Christians and be enabled to stand on tiptoe with joy, the author will feel that his labors have not been in vain. For whatever work is initiated by the Spirit has the glorious tendency and capacity to spread. May it spread far and wide is our prayer.

—J. T. SEAMANDS

1

The Divine Ambassador

I will send him unto you (John 16:7).

The Holy Spirit is the unknown Member of the Trinity. We know much about God the Father and much about God the Son, but relatively little about God the Holy Spirit. If the Apostle Paul were to come to many of our modern congregations and ask the same question that he asked of certain disciples in Ephesus many years ago, namely, "Did you receive the Holy Spirit when you believed?" he would probably receive the same answer that he received on that occasion—"No, we have not even heard that there is a Holy Spirit" (Acts 19:2, RSV). There is woeful ignorance of the Third Person of the Trinity in our churches today.

Some people—Christians at that—are afraid of the Holy Spirit. One preacher remarked, "I preach about God the Father and about Christ the Son, but I never preach about the Holy Spirit." When asked for the reason, he replied, "I'm afraid to preach about the Holy Spirit; it may lead to fanaticism."

Another preacher said to Dr. E. Stanley Jones on one occasion, "Every time you mention the Holy

Spirit, cold chills go up and down my spine." When Dr. Jones asked, "Why?" he replied, "I'm afraid of rampant emotionalism."

Suppose I receive a long-distance telephone call from a certain pastor and he says to me, "Brother Seamands, we want you to come to our church and preach a series of sermons, but please don't bring your wife along."

Naturally I would ask, "Why do you object to my wife coming along?"

He replies, "Well, we have heard that your wife has fits once in a while, and we're afraid she may have a fit in one of the services. We certainly can't afford to have that happen. I hope you understand."

I would certainly reply, "Sir, I don't know where you got this news. My wife *doesn't* have fits. That's someone else's wife you're talking about."

In like manner, when I hear someone attributing to the Holy Spirit that which is unseemly and ungracious, I feel like saying, "Sir, that's not the Holy Spirit you're talking about! that's some other spirit!"

Every truth may be perverted. The higher the truth, the greater the possibility of perversion. It is sad that some people have queered the doctrine of the Holy Spirit and have gone off into many tangents and extremes, but we want to be careful that in rejecting these perversions we do not reject the truth itself. We need to rid ourselves of false notions and prejudices, but at the same time we must hold on to the truth.

The Holy Spirit is a wonderful Person. We need to understand Him and know Him.

Jesus was more filled with the Holy Spirit than any person who ever walked upon the face of the earth, and He was the most radiant and balanced Personality the world has ever seen. We need not be afraid of the Holy Spirit. He will make us like Christ!

Let us begin our spiritual quest of the Holy Spirit by asking two simple questions: (1) Who is the Holy Spirit? (2) What is the ministry of the Holy Spirit?

I. Who Is the Holy Spirit?

First, let us approach the question *negatively,* so that we may push aside some of our false ideas about the Holy Spirit.

The Holy Spirit is *not a thing or an object.* He should never be referred to by the neuter pronoun "it."

Several years ago the Christians of Latin America were celebrating the festival of the Holy Spirit. In one congregation some members went from house to house, raising an offering "to put the Holy Spirit in their church." When they came to a certain home and explained their mission, the occupant of the house asked, "What is the Holy Spirit?"

The leader of the group replied, "Don't you know what the Holy Spirit is? You know that in every church above the altar there is the image of the dove. That dove is the Holy Spirit. In our church we do not have such an image. So we are raising money to have a sculptor fashion a beautiful dove which we can place over the altar. Then we will have the Holy Spirit in our church."

There people looked upon the Holy Spirit as some object to be seen. They may have been sincere, but they were grossly misled. The Holy Spirit is not a thing or an object.

The Holy Spirit is *not merely the divine life within us.* He is the Spirit of Life, to be sure, and quickens us from death unto life. But He is more than mere life.

A tree has life of a sort. But have you ever seen a tree with a college degree? Have you ever seen a stubborn tree? Have you ever seen a tree with its feelings hurt? The tree possesses life, but is not a person.

The Holy Spirit is *not merely the power of God at work in our lives.* He is not simply an impersonal force.

Gasoline is a source of power that drives our automobiles. But it has nothing to say about which direction or at what speed the car goes.

The Holy Spirit is the Source of spiritual power.

But He is more than power or some sort of influence emanating from God.

Looking at it positively, we must emphasize the fact that *the Holy Spirit is a Person*. Note that Jesus always referred to Him with the use of the personal pronoun, "He" or "Him." "I will send *him* unto you. . . . When *he* is come . . . *he* will guide you into all truth."

As a Person, the Holy Spirit possesses the three attributes of personality: intellect, will, and emotion.

The Holy Spirit has *intellect,* possessing all wisdom and knowledge. He knows, understands, and judges. Paul talks about "the mind of the Spirit" (Rom. 8:27). Jesus said to His disciples, "He shall teach you all things" (John 14:26).

The Holy Spirit has *will*. He decides, chooses, and commands. In the Book of the Acts we read how on several occasions the Holy Spirit commanded the disciples not to go into certain areas and to go into other areas. We read such phrases (RSV) as: "having been forbidden by the Holy Spirit," "being sent forth by the Holy Spirit," "bound in the Spirit," all of which testify that the Holy Spirit possesses will.

The Holy Spirit also has *emotion*. Paul admonishes us, "Grieve not the holy Spirit of God." You can't grieve an inanimate object. You can only grieve a person with feelings. Such emotions as love, joy, and peace are attributed to the indwelling presence of the Spirit in our lives.

The sum total of all these verses of Scripture dealing with the Holy Spirit reveals the truth that He is a self-conscious Being, possessing intellect, will, and emotion. The recognition of this fact will change our whole attitude toward the Spirit.

The Holy Spirit is a Person, but He is more than an ordinary person. You and I are persons, possessing intellect, will, and emotion. But we are human personalities, while the Holy Spirit is a divine Personality. He is a Member of the Holy Trinity, and thus possesses all the attributes of divinity. All the characteristics that we ascribe to God the Father and Christ the Son we can also ascribe to God the Holy Spirit. He is omnipotent, omniscient, omnipresent, holy, loving, and perfect. He is equal to God; He *is* God. He is a Member of the Holy Trinity.

The doctrine of the Trinity is a truth that is revealed by Scripture, but it is a mystery that transcends human reason.

A Muslim mullah (teacher) in Nigeria said to Dr. Harry Rimmer, Presbyterian minister who was visiting his country, "You Christians believe in three Gods. You talk about God the Father, God the Son, and God the Holy Spirit. But God is only One."

Dr. Rimmer said to the mullah, "Let me ask you something. Are you a living body? Are you a living soul? Are you a living spirit?" Receiving an affirmative answer on all three, Dr. Rimmer then asked the Muslim which of the three was himself.

The mullah replied, "All three!" but could explain no further.

The Christian evangelist then went on to point out that each one of us is a trinity on the human level, and yet we regard ourselves as one. Somehow, in some mysterious way beyond our comprehension, the Godhead is three and yet one.

A Muslim in India once said to me: "You Christians don't know mathematics. You say 'one plus one plus one equals one,' but it really equals three."

In reply I asked him, "How much is one times one times one?"

He answered, "One."

I said, "You see, I have proved the Trinity just as much as you have disproved it." The fact of the matter is, when we try to explain divine mysteries in human language, we get just so far and then find we can go no further.

The Holy Spirit is a Person, but more. He is a divine Person. This means that He possesses the attributes of personality in their perfection. He is Infinite Intellect, Perfect Will, and Perfect Emotion.

Our minds are human and therefore limited. We often fail to grasp the truth. But if we sit at the feet of the Divine Intellect, He will guide us into the truth and teach us concerning the deeper things of God.

Our wills are human and therefore weak. We often do the things we ought not to do, and leave undone the things that we should do. But if we surrender ourselves to the Divine Will, He will bolster our weak will and enable us to refrain from the things we ought not to do and to perform the duties we ought to do.

Our emotions are human and often mixed up. We hate the things we should love, and love the things we should hate. But if we surrender ourselves to the Divine Emotion, He will cleanse and redirect our emotions, so that we are enabled to hate the things that God hates and love the things that God loves.

Thus the truth of the divine Personality of the Holy Spirit has great significance for each one of us in his daily spiritual life. As someone has aptly put it: "If we try to understand all about the Holy Spirit, we will lose our minds; but if we try to live without Him, we will lose our souls."

II. WHAT IS THE MINISTRY OF THE HOLY SPIRIT?

The role of the Holy Spirit in His relationship to men is threefold:

First of all, *He is the divine Ambassador.* He is the Executive of the Godhead. He is God's Representative upon earth.

An ambassador is a very important person. He presents his credentials to the foreign power and then he is accepted and respected as the official representative of his government. When he speaks, he speaks not as an individual for himself, but on behalf of the entire nation from which he comes. All the authority and power of his government are back of him.

As the divine Ambassador, the Holy Spirit does not speak for himself. He speaks on behalf of God the Father and seeks primarily to glorify Christ the Son. And when He speaks, all the authority of the Godhead is back of Him.

In the role of Ambassador, the Holy Spirit does

three things. Jesus said: "And when he is come, he will reprove [convince] the world of sin, and of righteousness, and of judgment" (John 16:8).

He convinces (convicts) of *sin*. No man can really see himself as God sees him apart from the working of the Holy Spirit in his heart and mind. The Spirit lays bare the heart of man, exposes his sin, and pronounces him guilty before God. This is a disturbing experience for any man. He may lose his sleep or his appetite. He certainly loses his peace of mind. But the Holy Spirit shows man his sin only in order that man will seek the Saviour. As Sam Shoemaker once said, "Before the Holy Spirit can be the Comforter He has to be the Discomforter. He upsets us merely that He may set us up."

Several years ago I was conducting a mission to university students in the city of Trivandrum in south India. One morning a young medical student came to see me. In all sincerity he said, "I find difficulty in believing there is a God. Can you prove to me that God exists?"

So for the next hour or two I gave him all the rational arguments for the existence of God—the cosmological argument, the teleological argument, the moral argument, and the anthropological argument. I also used many verses from the Bible to reinforce these arguments. But at the end of a long discussion he was still unconvinced. However he did promise to attend the evening services and expose himself to the Word of God.

About two days later, just before I entered the church, the pastor handed me a note written by this young medical student. On it he had scribbled, "I think there is some truth in what you are saying. Please pray for me." The following evening when I finished my message and the congregation had dispersed, I noticed this young man was still seated in the church, his face buried in his hands. He seemed to be weeping. I went down and sat by his side. "What's the trouble?" I asked.

"Sir," he replied, "I'm a terrible sinner; please pray

for me." I prayed for him as best I knew how, and counseled him out of the Scriptures. Finally he prayed his own simple prayer, and I sensed very clearly the presence of God in our midst. Suddenly he looked up at me with a smile on his face, gripped me by the hand, and said, "Now I know there is a God. He's in my heart!"

I realized immediately that I had witnessed the gracious work of the Holy Spirit. What reason and argument could not do, He accomplished. He convicted this young man of sin and then led him to the Heavenly Father. Only the Spirit can do this.

Again, the Holy Spirit convicts of *righteousness*. He shows us that our own morality and good deeds are but filthy rags in the sight of God and that true righteousness is found only in Jesus Christ. He teaches us that righteousness is an obtainment and not an achievement. It is the gift of God and not the product of man.

A few years ago, when our family was making preparations to come home to the United States on furlough, one morning I was in the mission bungalow packing our trunks. For this menial task I had put on some old work clothes. My pants were stained with paint and grease; my shirt was worn and frayed. Suddenly there was a knock at the door and I went to see who it was. There stood an Indian gentleman, immaculate in his dress. He was the picture of neatness and cleanliness. Immediately I became aware of my dirty clothes and my untidiness, and I felt embarrassed in his presence, and began to make excuses for my appearance. The contrast was convincing.

In the same way, many of us are satisfied with our spiritual condition until the Holy Spirit places Christ, in all His perfection, before us. There, for the first time, we see absolute holiness. We immediately look at ourselves, with our sin and imperfection, and we feel embarrassed in His presence. We see how far we have fallen short of the glory of God. We now realize what true righteousness is and where it may be found. This illumination is the work of the Holy Spirit.

Then again, the Holy Spirit convicts man of the *judgment*. He reveals to us that the prince of this world, Satan, has already been judged by the death of our Lord Jesus Christ, and that we too, apart from the grace of God, stand condemned before the heavenly tribunal. He reminds us that one day each one will have to stand before the judgment bar of God and give an account of his deeds and words, his opportunities and privileges, his talents and possessions. We are all answerable to God. The Spirit makes this clear.

So as the divine Ambassador, convicting us of sin, righteousness, and judgment, the Holy Spirit is to be revered and heeded. He speaks with authority and finality.

In the second place, *the Holy Spirit is the divine Nurse*. He makes available to man what Christ made possible through His death.

A pastor in India gave me this illustration of the Trinity. He said: "I look upon God the Father as the divine Physician who examines man, the patient, and discovers that he has a fatal disease called sin. In keeping with the disease he prescribes the remedy. Christ, the Son, is like the technician who goes into the laboratory and actually prepares the remedy for the disease. He goes into the laboratory of Calvary and by His death and resurrection provides for the redemption of mankind. The Holy Spirit is like the nurse who actually delivers the remedy and nurses the patient back to health and strength. He takes all the love of God and all the grace of Christ and makes them personal to the individual who repents of his sin and puts his trust in the Saviour. That is, all that Jesus did *for* man the Holy Spirit now does *in* man."

We can't get along without the Physician or the laboratory Technician. Neither can we get along without the Nurse. We are absolutely dependent upon His ministry in this work of redemption. To reject Him is to reject our only source of help.

As the divine Ambassador the Holy Spirit is to be *respected*. As the divine Nurse, He is to be *received*.

In the third place, *the Holy Spirit is the divine*

Resident. Paul asks, "Know ye not that ye are the temple of God, and that the Spirit of God dwelleth in you?" (I Cor. 3:16)

There are two great mysteries in the Christian faith. One is that God would condescend to live *with* man in the person of His Son, Jesus Christ. The other is that God would condescend to live *in* man in the person of the Holy Spirit. To think that God would be willing to empty himself of His glory and power and come to earth to live as a man among men is truly beyond all human comprehension. To think that God, who is infinite and holy, would be willing to take up His abode in the heart of man, who is finite and sinful, is also beyond all human understanding. And yet it is true! God wills and longs to dwell in man.

In one of our mission boarding schools in India there was a young village lad who was always getting into mischief. Often the teacher would try to advise and correct him. One day when the boy did something wrong, as usual the teacher chided him, so in desperation the lad looked up into the face of his teacher and said, "Teacher, you are good and always do the right thing, and I seem to be bad and always do the wrong thing. If you could just crawl down inside of me and stay there, then I would always be good!"

How often in desperation we look up into the face of the Heavenly Father and say, "Lord, You are infinitely good and always do the right thing. I am evil and often do the wrong thing. If You would just get down inside of me and stay there, then I too could be good!"

But that is exactly what God wants to do. He wants to get deep down inside of us, in the person of the Holy Spirit, and make us like Christ. He wants to *take* us over and *make* us over. There, where the surgeon can't get with his knife or the psychiatrist with his probing, the Holy Spirit will dwell and work, controlling our thoughts and emotions, purifying our desires and motives, directing our wills and ambitions. And this is exactly what it means to be a Spirit-filled Christian. Not making a lot of resolutions or trying to live up to certain standards in our own strength, but receiving the Holy Spirit into the center of our personalities and allowing Him to cleanse and control and empower. True righteousness is not put on, but put in. To be a Christian means to have the Holy Spirit residing in your heart and mind.

Thus the Holy Spirit is God's greatest Gift to man, for in the Holy Spirit God is actually offering himself. What more can He give? It is like the bridegroom who has given many gifts to his intended bride—perfume, candy, flowers, wearing apparel, etc.—but now at the altar of the church he comes to the place where he makes the final gift of himself. Without the giving of himself all the other gifts would be meaningless, but with it they find their fulfillment. And so God, who has given us many gifts—life, health, strength, forgiveness, peace, comfort, joy, etc. —now comes to the place where He wants to give us the greatest gift of all, the gift of Himself. He is not satisfied with anything less; neither should we be.

But so often we miss the point in our spiritual lives. We seek gifts and blessings but do not receive the Giver Himself. We seek *presents* rather than the *Presence*.

When I was a missionary in India I used to leave home on frequent and extended evangelistic tours. I made it a practice to bring home each time some little gift for my youngest daughter—a box of crayons, a paint book, a book of stories, a toy, or some novelty. Whenever I reached home there would be that moment of excitement when I would open up the suitcase and present the gift to my little redheaded girl.

On one such trip I had been into the interior, preaching in small villages where there were no stores or bazaars. I was forced to return empty-handed. When I arrived back at the house, as usual little Sandra rushed up, threw her arms around me, and asked excitedly, "Daddy, what present have you brought me this time?"

For a moment I was silent, but then I said, "Honey, I'm sorry, but I was not able to buy anything for you this time, but I'll tell you something. I've been away from home a long time and have been very homesick for my little girl, so this time instead of a gift I have just brought myself. Isn't that a wonderful gift? Aren't you glad to see your daddy?"

I could see the look of disappointment spread over Sandy's face. Her lips quivered and her eyes moistened a bit. Then she said, "Yes, Daddy, I'm glad you are home; but why, why didn't you bring me a present?"

Many of us are like that. The Heavenly Father comes to us and says, "Son, Daughter, I've given you many gifts, but now I offer myself to you. I want to live in you. This is the most wonderful thing I can do for you." And like little children we look up into His face and say, "But, Lord, I thought You would bring another gift!"

And so we go on seeking presents and miss the glorious Presence. We seek gifts and miss the Giver.

We should seek *Him,* not *it.* We should receive the Empowerer, not just a little bit of power. We should receive the Sanctifier, not just cleansing. We should receive the Giver of joy, not just a feeling of joy. We should receive the Comforter, not just a little bit of comfort. Receive *Him* and you've got *it.* Without *Him* you cannot have *it.* All the gifts of God are fulfilled in the blessed person of the Holy Spirit Himself.

In the days of the Roman Empire there was a wealthy Roman senator who had only one son. The father made out his will, leaving everything to the boy, whom he loved so dearly. But as days went by, the son became more and more disobedient and quarrelsome, and finally one day in a fit of anger he left home and was not heard of for many years. In desperation the heartbroken father rewrote his will, leaving everything he had to a trusted slave—with just one provision: if the son returned home, he could choose one thing, and only one, out of the entire inheritance.

On hearing of his father's death, the wayward son returned home, only to learn of the change in the will. Everything now belonged to his father's slave. But he could choose one thing, only one, out of the whole estate. The young man stood debating within himself what he should choose. Should he choose a house in which to live, a field which he could cultivate, or a part of the business? Then in a flash of inspiration he pointed to the slave and said, "I'll take him!" And in choosing the slave he got back his whole inheritance, for it was wrapped up in the person of the slave.

In the same way, when we receive the person of the Holy Spirit, we receive the whole inheritance of Christ. All the gifts are wrapped up in Him.

God is offering himself. He can give nothing higher! Don't settle for anything less!

2

Resident and President

Be not drunk with wine, wherein is excess; but be filled with the Spirit (Eph. 5:18).

In these words of the Apostle Paul we find a comparison, a contrast, and a command.

There is, first of all, the *comparison*. Like wine, the fulness of the Holy Spirit produces unnatural boldness, utterance, power, and optimism. The man with his drink is afraid of no one; his stammering tongue is loosed; he feels equal to anything; failure is unthinkable. Such are some of the effects on the timid believer filled with the Holy Spirit.

Then there is the *contrast* between the human stimulus, wine, and the divine stimulus, the Holy Spirit. There is the possibility of excess in drinking wine, but not in partaking of the Holy Spirit. And whereas drunkenness leads to folly, the fulness of the Holy Spirit leads to wisdom. Whereas drunkenness leads to riot, the fulness of the Holy Spirit leads to self-control. Whereas drunkenness leads to hellishness, the fulness of the Holy Spirit leads to holiness.

Finally, there is the *command*. It is really a two-fold command. One is negative: "Be not drunk with

wine." The other is positive: "Be filled with the Spirit."
Isn't it strange that we place so much emphasis on
the negative command but almost entirely overlook
the positive command?

Some time ago the world-famous evangelist, Dr.
Billy Graham, was being shown through a church by
some of the elders. In the conversation one of them
said: "We had a very tragic experience in our church
recently. We had to excommunicate one of the members for coming to church in a somewhat intoxicated
condition."

Billy Graham asked: "What discipline do you take
against a member who comes to church *not* filled with
the Holy Spirit?"

Somewhat puzzled, the elder said: "I don't understand your question."

"Well," said Mr. Graham, "you know the Scripture—'Be not drunk with wine . . . but be filled with
the Spirit.' Now if somebody disobeys the first command and gets drunk, you excommunicate him. But
what about somebody who fails to obey the second
command and does not receive the fulness of the Holy
Spirit? How do you discipline *him?*"

The Church treats drunkenness as a serious offense,
and rightly so, but it is equally tragic for its members
to neglect the fulness of the Holy Spirit!

The command to be filled with the Spirit is just as
definite as the command to repent or to believe on the
Lord Jesus Christ.

The early Christian Church placed the emphasis on
the Spirit-filled life. In obedience to the command of
Christ to tarry in the city of Jerusalem until they be
endued with power from on high, the disciples tarried
in an upper room, prayed, and surrendered themselves,
until the Day of Pentecost, when "they were all filled
with the Holy Spirit." From then on, that became the
norm of Christian experience and life in the Early
Church. The phrase "full of the Holy Spirit" is used
over and over again in the Book of Acts.

When the time came to choose the first deacons of
the church of Jerusalem, one of the important spiritual

qualifications for these men was that they should be filled with the Holy Spirit (Acts 6:3). When Philip conducted a great revival in Samaria and many turned to the Lord, the apostles in Jerusalem sent up Peter and John for the express purpose of laying hands on the new converts that they might receive the baptism with the Holy Spirit (Acts 8:14-17). When Ananias came to see the new convert, Saul, in Damascus, he said, "Brother Saul, the Lord Jesus . . . has sent me that you may regain your sight and be filled with the Holy Spirit" (Acts 9:17, RSV). Later on when Paul came to the city of Ephesus and found certain disciples there, the first question he asked was, "Have you received the Holy Ghost [Spirit] since you believed?" (Acts 19:2).

All these examples testify to the fact that the Early Church placed the emphasis on the fulness of the Holy Spirit.

Dr. Halford Luccock, former professor of homiletics at Yale Divinity School, loved to tell this incident from his personal experience. One day a policeman friend of his stopped him in the midst of street traffic and asked, "What is the degree which many preachers have which makes them doctors?"

Dr. Luccock answered, "It is usually a D.D.—Doctor of Divinity. Why did you ask?"

"Well," said the policeman, "down at the police station that is the most common entry on the charge sheet. To us it means 'Drunk and Disorderly.' So when I saw 'Rev. So-and-So, D.D.' I was naturally curious."

Dr. Luccock pulled away safely before reeling from that blow, but when he reached home he began to meditate on the policeman's words. Suddenly it came to him that those were the very same charges brought against the early disciples on the Day of Pentecost. The crowd said, "These men are drunk with wine." Later on the disciples were dragged before the rulers of the city and were charged with being disorderly. "These men have turned the world upside down," shouted their accusers. And then in his inimitable way Dr. Luccock commented, "How I would love to stand before every congregation in the church and say in most solemn tones, 'Now with the authority invested in me as a minister of the Gospel, I confer upon each and every one of you the degree of D.D.—drunk and disorderly.' That, in figurative terms, is a very honorary degree, a degree that every Christian should possess."

The early Christians had this degree. How we need it today! And so the Pauline exhortation, "Be filled with the Spirit," comes to us with renewed force these days.

But what does it mean to be filled with the Spirit?

Before we can answer this question, we have to step back and ask and answer a preliminary question: What is the relationship of the Holy Spirit to every believer? We have already noted the relationship of the Holy Spirit to the unregenerated person. His role is that of Ambassador; convicting the sinner of sin, righteousness, and the judgment. But what is His relationship to the person who has repented of his sins and put his trust in the Lord Jesus Christ as his Saviour? For the answer we turn to Scripture.

First of all, *every believer is born of the Spirit.* Jesus said to Nicodemus, "Except a man be born of water and of the Spirit, he cannot enter into the kingdom of God" (John 3:5). When a man accepts Christ as his personal Saviour, he is quickened by the Holy Spirit from death unto life. He is born again. He becomes a new creature in Christ Jesus. Old things pass away and all things become new. He becomes a child of God and enters into the family of God. We commonly speak of this experience in such terms as the new birth, conversion, or regeneration. Each term emphasizes a different aspect of the same spiritual experience.

Again, *every believer is assured by the Holy Spirit.* In his Epistle to the Romans Paul writes, "The Spirit itself beareth witness with our spirit, that we are the children of God" (Rom. 8:16). This is the inner assurance that every born-again person has that he has been accepted by Christ, that his sins are forgiven, and that he is a child of God. John Wesley spoke of this as "the witness of the Spirit." It is something subjective, within the soul of a person, but at the same time very real. It is a conviction wrought in the human spirit by the Spirit of God.

Third, *every believer is sealed by the Holy Spirit*. In his letter to the Ephesian church Paul writes, "Ye were sealed with that holy Spirit of promise" (Eph. 1:13; see also 4:30). To the Corinthian Christians he wrote much the same thing (II Cor. 1:22). In Greek culture the seal was a legal mark of ownership on a closure to prevent tampering. In the same way the Holy Spirit seals the believer, that is, puts His stamp of ownership upon him, so that he becomes the special possession of God.

At the same time the Holy Spirit becomes the *Guarantee* or *Earnest* of our final redemption. This was a business term used in Paul's day with the same significance as the modern business term *down payment*. The word is illuminating, for it states that the Holy Spirit is the Guarantee of our inheritance until we acquire possession of it. A more common illustration would be the engagement ring or other symbol which is the token of marriage promised until the marriage is complete. Thus the Holy Spirit in the heart of the believer is the heavenly Token or the Down Payment on the mansion in glory.

Fourth, *every believer is baptized into the body of Christ by the Holy Spirit*. This is a truth stated by Paul in I Cor. 12:13—"For by one Spirit are we all baptized into one body." It's like a mason taking a brick and placing it into the wall which he is building. The brick now becomes a part of the wall. In like manner the Holy Spirit places the believer in the body of Christ, that is, the Church of Christ, and now the believer becomes a member of the Church Universal.

Finally, *every believer is indwelt by the Holy Spirit*. Paul wrote to the Christians at Corinth: "Know ye not that ye are the temple of God, and that the Spirit of God dwelleth in you?" (I Cor. 3:16). This he wrote to Christians who were far from perfect. We must not make the mistake of thinking that the Person of the Holy Spirit is not involved when a man is converted or born again—that the Holy Spirit is active only in a later experience of grace. The moment a man receives Christ as his Saviour, he receives the indwelling presence of the Holy Spirit. No man could live the Christian life for a moment without this Presence. Paul said, "If any man have not the Spirit of Christ, he is none of his" (Rom. 8:9). Every child of God is inhabited by the Holy Spirit.

The indwelling presence of the Holy Spirit is the secret of the Christian life—not our strivings, our resolutions, our efforts, nor our determination, but the Spirit of Christ living in and through us. He takes us over and makes us over. This is what it means to be a Christian.

However, having said all of this—that the true believer is born of the Spirit, assured by the Spirit, sealed by the Spirit, baptized by the Spirit into the body of Christ, and inhabited by the Spirit—we must be quick to add that not every believer is *filled* with the Spirit. It is one thing to be *born* of the Spirit and another thing to be *filled* with the Spirit. The Holy Spirit may be *living* in our hearts, but not completely *ruling* in our lives. Christ may be *Saviour,* but not *Sovereign.* The Spirit may be a *Resident,* but not *President.*

As I go from place to place conducting missionary and evangelistic services, I am often the guest in some layman's home or in the parsonage. When I arrive, the host usually receives me graciously and says, "Brother Seamands, we are glad to have you in our home. Please make yourself completely at home. Here is the bedroom; here is the bathroom; here is the sitting room. Feel free to play the piano or turn on the TV set. Let us know if there is anything you need."

Now what does all this mean? It means that certain rooms and facilities in the house have been set apart for my convenience. It doesn't mean that I can walk into every room in the house at will and help myself to anything I see, or that I can boss the various members of the household according to my desires. I am in the house, but in the limited role of a *guest*. But when I come back to my own home in Wilmore, Kentucky, the situation is different. I am no longer just a guest in the house; I am master of the home. I can go into any room in the house at will. I claim the house and all its furnishings as my own.

This is a spiritual parable. There are some people who have opened the door of their hearts and allowed the Spirit of Christ to walk across the threshold of their lives. But they say to Him, "Lord, You can go into this room, and this one, and this one, but not into that one over there. That's my private office. No admission without permission." And so, though the Holy Spirit is present in the house and certainly has done much for the owner of the house, He is there in the limited role of a Guest. He does not have full control.

To be filled with the Spirit means that the child of God has opened up every room in the house to the Spirit's free entry, and more, has handed over the whole bunch of keys into His hand. It means that the Spirit is not only a Guest but is the Master of the house.

As another illustration, consider the relationship of Lyndon B. Johnson to the United States. A few years ago he was the senator from Texas, *in* the U.S.A. but in the limited role of a representative. Then later he became the vice-president of the United States, still in the States but in a more responsible relationship. Then, however, Lyndon B. Johnson became president of the United States, still in the same country but in the role of the chief executive.

To be filled with the Holy Spirit means to come into the closest possible relationship with Him, where He is not only the Representative of the Godhead, but is now the Chief Executive. He is not only a Resident, but is now President. Christ is not only Saviour, but is now Sovereign.

This intimate relationship with the Master through the person of the Holy Spirit is masterfully pictured in the familiar words of Rev. 3:20, "Behold, I stand at the door and knock: if any man hear my voice, and open the door, I will come in to him, and will sup with him, and he with me." Here we have the threefold relationship of Christ to men. To some He is the Stranger, on the outside, knocking, seeking for entrance. To those who have accepted Him as Saviour, He is on the inside, but in the limited role of a Guest. He is seated at the household table. He sups with the owner. But to those who have made a full surrender of themselves He becomes the Master of the house. Now he sits at the table as the Host, and the believer sups with Him. This is the intimate relationship that Christ desires with every child of His.

Thus it is clear that the main reason why every child of God is not filled with the Holy Spirit is that he has not made a full surrender to God of every part of his being and every aspect of his daily living. As a result the individual, instead of being filled with the Spirit (capital *S*), is partially filled with some other spirit (small *s*). He may be partially filled with the spirit of pride, and so the Holy Spirit, who is the Spirit of humility, cannot fill that life. Or he may be partially filled with the spirit of selfishness, and therefore the Holy Spirit, who is the Spirit of sacrifice, is unable to fill that life. Or again the individual may be partially filled with the spirit of hatred or resentment, thus making it impossible for the Holy Spirit of love to fill his heart.

So in order to be filled with the Holy Spirit the believer must be willing to be emptied of all un-Christlike attitudes and desires. Note, I said he must be *willing to be emptied;* not, he must empty himself. That is a mistake many people make. They try to empty or cleanse themselves of these unholy attitudes, but that is impossible. All they can do is to be willing to be emptied or cleansed, and the Holy Spirit will do the actual work.

There are two ways to rid a glass of water of its contents. One way is to turn the glass upside down and pour out the water. The other way is to pour mercury (or some such substance heavier than water and incompatible with it) into the glass and it will automatically displace the water. Now it is impossible to look down into our hearts and, seeing the resentment, bitterness, hatred, jealousy, impurity, etc., just take our hearts like a glass, turn them upside down, and pour out the contents. The only thing we can do is to allow the Holy Spirit to fill and permeate every part of our being; and as He does, He automatically displaces all these un-Christlike attitudes and desires. In other words, this is an act that we cannot do for ourselves, but must permit the Holy Spirit to do in us.

This surrender on the part of the believer and the consequent filling on the part of the Spirit are the secret of sanctification in the Christian life. For where the Holy Spirit is, there will be holiness. No impurity can remain where He has perfect control. Thus sanctification is not merely an impersonal experience, an "it" that you get; it is primarily a relationship to a Person, the Holy Spirit. As long as the Christian maintains this intimate relationship with the Spirit by a constant attitude of surrender and obedience, so long will the Spirit fill and permeate every part of his being and keep on cleansing from moment to moment. But the moment the Christian mars his relationship by self-will or disobedience, at that moment unholy attitudes and desires may enter his life and bring spiritual defeat.

It is like a pebble that lies on the bottom of the mountain stream. As long as it remains in the stream, the water washes over it and keeps it clean. The moment you take the pebble out of the stream and place it on the dry ground, it is liable to become dirty. So as long as we remain "in the Spirit," we are spiritually safe and clean; the moment we get out of the Spirit, we are in danger of becoming unclean. The secret of purity is to maintain the relationship.

Likewise, this surrender and the resultant infilling are the secret of power in the Christian life. Like purity, power is not an "it" that you receive, or just an impersonal force; it is a relationship to the Holy Spirit, who is the Empowerer. The Holy Spirit doesn't wrap up 50 or 100 pounds of power and hand it over to us, but as He fills and permeates us, He also empowers us. Now that we are fully surrendered to His will and are completely under His control, His power can flow freely and fully through our lives at the moment it is needed. All the hindrances and blocks to the flow of His power have been removed. As long as we maintain this relationship by surrender and obedience, the power will flow. But if we mar the relationship, the power will be blocked. Receive *Him* and you've got *it*. You can't have *it* without *Him*.

The gateway into the Spirit-filled life is, therefore, the gateway of full surrender. The Holy Spirit gives himself in His fulness only to those who give themselves in their entirety.

An Englishman giving his testimony before a group said, "Up until now there has been a constitutional monarchy in my spiritual life. Christ has been King, while I have been the prime minister, making all the decisions. But now I have resigned from my position and have made Christ King, Prime Minister, and Lord of all."

When we are willing for Christ to be Lord, then the Holy Spirit will fill us.

Just a word about this matter of surrender or consecration. Many of us, when we come to make our surrender, do something like this. We take a sheet of paper, write at the top, "My Consecration," then begin to fill in the page with our resolutions—"I will read my Bible and pray every day. I will attend Sunday school and church services regularly every Sunday. I will teach a Sunday school class or sing in the choir if I am requested to do so. I will give my tithe regularly to the church. I will witness for Christ whenever I have an opportunity to do so." And so on down the page. Then we sign our names at the bottom and hand over the sheet of consecration to the Lord.

The Master very tenderly, yet deliberately, hands back the sheet, and says to us, "Son, Daughter, that's not what I want." And then handing us a blank sheet of paper, He says, "Just sign your name at the bottom. I'll fill in the rest!"

That's consecration. Not our telling what we will

do for Him, but signing ourselves over to Him and letting Him tell us what He wants us to do. It may take Him five, ten, twenty, or fifty years to fill in the sheet, but that's His business. If you're a young person, five years down the line He may call you to be a foreign missionary. The moment He calls, you will say, "Lord, I've signed at the bottom. I'm willing to go." Twenty years down the line He may ask you to go through some difficult trial. You will say, "I've signed at the bottom. Thy will be done."

But you say, "That's asking too much. The price is too high. If I did that I would be at the mercy of Christ." But let me remind you that you are not surrendering to a cruel tyrant who wants to make life miserable for you and order you around at his whim. You are surrendering to a loving, gracious Lord who desires nothing but the best for you. He wants to make something out of your life for His honor and glory and the blessing of mankind. You never need to be afraid of surrendering to Him. It is true you will not be able to have your way in everything, but you will find that His way is the best way—always!

Is the price too high? Remember, as you surrender your all to Him—your *little* all—He gives His all to you—His *big* all. When you are willing to take a blank sheet, sign your name at the bottom, then hand it over to Him and say, "Lord, You fill it in. You tell me what to do," then Christ takes a blank check on the bank of heaven, signs His name at the bottom, and says, "You fill it in. All the blessings of heaven are yours for the asking." Tell me, who gets the best of this transaction?

Several years ago in Memphis, Tennessee, it was my privilege to have lunch one Sunday noon with Mr. Horace Hull, co-owner of the Hull-Dobbs Ford dealership, one of the largest in the United States. During the conversation he told me a story which I have never forgotten.

Mr. Hull told how he and his family had driven down into the state of Georgia one weekend to visit some friends. As they were driving back over a narrow, mountainous road through a heavy downpour, suddenly they passed a family—father, mother, and five small children—trudging along the highway in the rain. They were holding two or three sheets over their heads, but still they were drenched to the skin.

Mr. Hull stopped the car and called out to them, "Why are you walking in this awful rain?"

The man slowly answered, "Sir, our house burned down just a few hours ago. We lost everything. So we are going over the hill to the house of a friend, trying to find a place to stay until we can make some other arrangements."

Mr. Hull's heart was touched with pity, so he reached into his pocket, pulled out a five-dollar bill, handed it to the mother, and said, "Here, take this and use it, and may God bless you."

But as he started on down the highway his conscience began to smite him. It said, "You're a miser. Here these people have nothing, and you have so much. All you gave them was a five-dollar bill. Can't you do better than that?"

So Mr. Hull pulled up alongside the highway, stopped his car, and turned his hat upside down on the seat beside him. Then reaching into his billfold he took out all the cash he had and placed it in the hat. He turned to his wife and said, "Honey, how much money do you have with you? I want you to put it all in the hat." He turned to his daughter and the Negro maid and asked them to do the same. The total collection came to about a hundred dollars. Then Mr. Hull turned the car around and started back toward the destitute family. They were still trudging along in the rain.

He pulled up alongside and called out to the mother, "Ma'am, do you have that five-dollar bill I gave you a little while ago?"

She said, "Yes."

"Well," said Mr. Hull, "I want you to give it back to me."

A look of pain went across the mother's face as if to say, What sort of a man are you anyway? You just gave me the money and now you're asking me to give it back. But without arguing she reached into her blouse, pulled out the five-dollar bill, and handed it back to him.

Mr. Hull said, "Here, put it into this hat." When she had done so, he continued, "Now hold out both hands." And as she put out her cupped hands, he turned the hat over, poured the contents into her hands, returning even the five-dollar bill he had originally given her, and said with a smile, "This is all I have with me. Take it all and use it. May God bless you."

When I heard this story, I thought, That's exactly what God wants to do for each one of us. He comes to us and says, "Son, Daughter, do you have that life I have given you?"

"Yes, Lord."

"Well, I want you to give it back to Me."

"But, Lord, I only have one life and it is short at that. How can I give it back?"

But He insists, "I want you to give it back to Me."

And here's the marvel of it all. The moment we give our lives back to Him, He says to us, "Here, you have given your all. Now take My all." And so saying He fills us completely with His Spirit until all His peace, and all His joy, and all His power become ours. Not only that, but He hands back the life that we offered to Him and it becomes a new life, redeemed and transformed for His glory. We are on tiptoe with joy.

We surrender, and He fills. This is the secret of the Spirit-filled life.

"Be filled with the Spirit."

3

The Baptism with Fire

I indeed baptize you with water unto repentance: but he that cometh after me is mightier than I, whose shoes I am not worthy to bear: he shall baptize you with the Holy Ghost, and with fire (Matt. 3:11).

There are two baptisms mentioned in this passage: the baptism with water unto repentance, and the baptism with the Holy Spirit and fire.

It will help us to distinguish between these two baptisms if we remember in each case the agent, the subject, and the element of the baptism. In the first baptism, the agent is the minister of God, the subject is the repenting sinner, and the element is water. Thus the minister baptizes with water the individual who confesses and forsakes his sin. In the second baptism, the Agent is Christ, the subject is the child of God, and the element is the Holy Spirit. That is, Christ baptizes the believer with His Spirit.

We must also be careful to distinguish between the baptism by the Holy Spirit and the baptism *with* the Holy Spirit. In I Cor. 12:13 the Apostle Paul instructs us that "by one Spirit are we all baptized into one body." In this baptism the Agent is the Holy Spirit, the subject is the believer, and the element is the body —that is, the Church—of Christ. This is the baptism *by* the Holy Spirit. In the baptism spoken of in the text, the Agent is Christ and the element is the Holy Spirit. This is the baptism *with* the Holy Spirit.

It is a tragedy that in churches today so much emphasis is placed on the baptism with water while the baptism with the Holy Spirit is almost totally neglected. People are so careful to have their children baptized, or to receive baptism themselves, but go on through the Christian life, year after year, without the all-important baptism with the Holy Spirit. They are more concerned that the minister of the church should baptize them than that Christ himself should administer His baptism!

The importance of this baptism with the Holy Spirit is seen in the fact that it is mentioned in each one of the Gospel narratives and also in the Book of the Acts of the Apostles. Study the verses in Matt. 3:11; Mark 1:8; Luke 3:16; John 1:33; and Acts 1:5. There are very few teachings that are mentioned so unanimously in the narrative portion of the New Testament.

The key to the understanding of this text is in the word "fire." Fire is one of the many symbols of the Holy Spirit that are used in the Scriptures. In the Old Testament there is the symbol of air or *breath*. The Holy Spirit is the Breath of God within us, signifying the life-giving ministry of the Spirit. Then there is the symbol of *oil,* which signifies the anointing of the individual by the Holy Spirit for a particular task. In the New Testament we have the symbol of *water.* Jesus said, "Except a man be born of water and of the Spirit, he cannot enter into the kingdom of God." Water here signifies the washing away of our sins. Finally we have the symbol of *fire,* which is perhaps the most dramatic and picturesque of all the symbols. It signifies the refining and empowering ministry of the Holy Spirit.

Walking along a path in the foothills of the Himalaya Mountains with an Indian minister a few years ago, I received one of the finest analogies of the Trinity that I have ever heard. My colleague said to me:

"I like to think of the Trinity in this way. God the Father is like the great sun up in the heavens. The sun is the source of light and heat and life. Even though it is very distant, it is so bright that we cannot look at it with the naked eye. Likewise, God is the Source of all spiritual light, warmth, and life. He is so majestic that no man can look upon Him. Sometimes He seems very distant.

"Jesus Christ is like the rays of the sun, which bring to us the light and the warmth of the sun and make it seem very close. Jesus was God in human flesh. We were able to look upon Him and see the glory of the Father. He made God seem very close and real to us.

"The Holy Spirit is like a magnifying glass, which, if you place it out in the sun over a sheet of paper, will concentrate the light and heat of the sun on one spot and set the sheet on fire. Likewise the Holy Spirit concentrates all the divine grace and power upon the individual who is receptive and sets him ablaze for God."

How true this is! The Holy Spirit is like a magnifying glass that sets us afire. No wonder the Scriptures speak of this baptism by Christ as the baptism "with fire."

Scientists tell us that fire contains three distinct rays. First there is the *actinic ray* that produces chemical change, that tempers steel and turns wood to ashes. Second, there is the *caloric ray* that produces heat. And third, there is the *luminiferous ray* that produces light.

This information gives us a clue to the working of the Holy Spirit in our lives. The fire of the Holy Spirit *burns up,* producing purity; it *burns within,* producing power; and it *burns on and on*—perpetually. Let us examine these three aspects.

I. THE HOLY SPIRIT BURNS UP

Sin is twofold in its nature. It resides in the *action* and also in the *attitude*. It is in the *outer conduct* as well as in the *inner character*. It is a matter of *transgression* as well as of *disposition*. There are the sins of the *flesh* and the sins of the *spirit*.

This fact is revealed through the Scriptures. For example, in the Ten Commandments, God says, "Thou shalt not steal." But He also says, "Thou shalt not covet." Stealing is an outer action, but covetousness is an inner attitude. A man covets in his heart and then goes out to steal with his hands. Both are violations of the commandments of God.

In his great prayer of penitence (Ps. 51), David cries out in anguish, "Blot out my transgressions." Then he goes on to pray, "Create in me a clean heart, O God." David realized that his outer sins of adultery and murder came from an inner sinful condition.

In the Sermon on the Mount, Jesus said, "Ye have heard that it was said by them of old time, Thou shalt not kill . . . but I say unto you, That whosoever is angry with his brother without a cause shall be in danger of the judgment" (Matt. 5:21-22). Anger or hatred is an attitude of the mind. Murder is an outer act. A man first hates and then goes out to kill.

Jesus also said in this sermon, "Ye have heard that it was said by them of old time, Thou shalt not commit adultery: but I say unto you, That whosoever looketh on a woman to lust after her hath committed adultery with her already in his heart" (Matt. 5:27-28). Lust is an inner disposition of the heart. Adultery is an outer action. A man lusts in his heart and then commits the act of adultery.

In his parable of the prodigal son or, more correctly, the prodigal sons, Jesus again brings out the twofold nature of sin. The younger son stands for the sins of the flesh, the sins of transgression. He was guilty of gluttony, drunkenness, licentiousness, and adultery. The elder son stands for the sins of the spirit, the sins of the disposition. He exhibited the inner attitudes of jealousy, self-righteousness, anger, unconcern, and an unforgiving spirit.

In his First Epistle, the Apostle John very clearly distinguishes between sins and sin. The plural form signifies outer sinful actions. The singular form signifies the inner sinful condition, the principle of sin.

And so, throughout Scripture, we can clearly trace the twofold nature of sin.

This fact is also seen in the lives of the disciples of Jesus. When Jesus called them, they forsook their occupations and their professions, and followed Him joyfully. Living in fellowship with Him from day to day, their lives were marvelously transformed, so that Jesus in His high priestly prayer testifies concerning them before the Father: "They have kept thy word. . . . the words which thou gavest me . . . they have received . . . and they have believed that thou didst send me. They are not of the world" (John 17:6, 8, 16). On another occasion Jesus said to His disciples, "Rejoice, because your names are written in heaven" (Luke 10:20). They were, without doubt, converted, regenerated men, delivered from the sins of transgression.

But as we look more closely into the lives of the disciples, we see that they were often defeated by the sins of the disposition. Sometimes they exhibited the spirit of *pride*. One time they disputed among themselves as to who would be the greatest. So Jesus placed a child in their midst and reminded them that "he that is least among you all, the same shall be great" (Luke 9:48). Mark records these added words, "If any man desire to be first, the same shall be last of all, and servant of all" (Mark 9:35).

At times they exhibited the spirit of *self-seeking*. James and John once came to Jesus and made the request that He would grant them the privilege of sitting, one on the right hand and the other on the left when He established His kingdom. Jesus rebuked them and reminded them that, while they were seeking for thrones and scepters, He was on His way to the Cross (Mark 10:35-40).

On this same occasion, when the other disciples heard what James and John had requested, they exhibited the spirit of *jealousy* and became displeased with these two brethren. Again Jesus had to remind the whole group that "whosoever will be great among you, shall be your minister" (Mark 10:43).

At times the disciples displayed a spirit of *anger* and *revenge*. Once while passing through a village of Samaria they sought hospitality for their Master and for themselves, but the Samaritans turned them down. Then James and John came to Jesus and said, "Lord, wilt thou that we command fire to come down from heaven, and consume them, even as Elias did?" And Jesus rebuked them saying, "Ye know not what manner of spirit ye are of. For the Son of man is not come to destroy men's lives, but to save them" (Luke 9:54-56).

Finally, on the night of the Crucifixion, the disciples exhibited the spirit of *fear* and *cowardice*. Peter denied his Lord three times. The others fled and hid themselves. Even after the Resurrection they were hiding behind closed doors for fear of the Jews (John 20:19).

All of these illustrations clearly point out that sin is twofold in its nature, and that we need deliverance not only from our outward sinful actions but also from our inner sinful dispositions.

Consequently, the ministry of the Holy Spirit is twofold. In *regeneration,* the Holy Spirit acts like *water,* cleansing away the guilt of our outer transgressions. In sanctification, He acts like *fire,* purging away our inner impurity and refining our dispositions. Both ministries are essential to the full redemption of man.

In the year 1665 the Great Plague broke out in the city of London. Hundreds died of this dread disease. Each morning the cleanup squads went through the streets with their carts, shouting, "Throw out the dead," and they took the bodies outside the city and disposed of them. Nothing could stop the onward march of this "black death." But a few months later, fire suddenly broke out in one part of the city. It started with one house, swept through the whole street, and devastated a vast section of London before it finally spent itself. History calls this "the great fire of

London." But what the medical skill of the day could not do, the fire speedily accomplished. Its flames swept through the crevices and hidden places, destroying the rats and the fleas, and brought to a halt the onward march of the plague.

There is only one remedy for the plague of sin in the human heart, and that is the refining fire of the Holy Spirit. He can cleanse us from our jealousy, and selfishness, and anger, and hatred, and lust—and help us to become Christlike, not only in our actions, but also in our reactions; not only in our outer deportment but in our inner disposition. The fire of the Holy Spirit burns up the dross, producing purity.

The Apostle Peter, in describing this refining ministry of the Holy Spirit, said to the members of the first Christian council in Jerusalem: "And God, which knoweth the hearts, bare them witness, giving them the Holy Ghost, even as he did unto us; and put no difference between us and them, purifying their heart by faith" (Acts 15:8-9).

II. THE HOLY SPIRIT BURNS WITHIN

Jesus described the second result of the baptism with the Holy Spirit when He said to His disciples, just before His ascension: "Ye shall receive power, after that the Holy Ghost is come upon you: and ye shall be witnesses unto me both in Jerusalem, and in all Judaea, and in Samaria, and unto the uttermost part of the earth" (Acts 1:8). This is also clearly defined when He gave them His final command: "Tarry ye in the city of Jerusalem, until ye be endued with power from on high" (Luke 24:29).

There is a line drawn through the New Testament and it is drawn at Pentecost. On one side of that line are spiritual inadequacy, moral fumbling, denial, and defeat. It is all very sub-Christian. Picture that little group of disciples huddled together in an upper room in Jerusalem. If they looked back, there was the Crucifixion with all its horror and tragedy. The shame of it revived within them. If they looked forward, there was the incredible assignment to go into all the world and preach the gospel to every creature. They had the message, but they didn't have the courage to proclaim it. If they looked within, there were discouragement and defeat. Fears lurked, jealousies festered, doubts assailed, and cowardice hung like a millstone about their necks.

But in the midst of all this, two things held them steady. One was an event; the other was a promise. First there was the Resurrection. Slow to believe it at first, they were now convinced of its reality. Their Master was alive! Then there was the promise, "Ye shall receive power, after that the Holy Ghost has come upon you." The Master had given His word; He would never fail them.

On the Day of Pentecost that promise passed into fulfillment, and the record tells us that "they were all filled with the Holy Ghost."

Now what do we see? On the other side of the line there is spiritual adequacy, moral certainty, the power of a redemptive offense, spiritual contagion, a plus sign. The cringing became conquering; the cowardly became courageous; the vacillating became dynamic; the weak and defeated became victorious. It is all so truly Christian.

Look, for example, at the marvelous change wrought in the life and ministry of the Apostle Peter. Just a few weeks previous to Pentecost, Peter didn't have the courage to acknowledge his Lord before a simple maidservant or an ordinary Roman soldier. Three times he denied his Lord. But on the Day of Pentecost he had the courage to stand before the crowds of Jerusalem, charge them with the guilt of the Crucifixion, and call them to repentance.

Someone has described this change wrought in Peter in this picturesque way. On the night of the Crucifixion it was Peter *near the fire.* He followed afar off and warmed himself by the fire. Then it was Peter *in the fire,* when he failed to live up to his boast and denied his Lord and got into trouble. But on the Day of Pentecost it was Peter *on fire,* baptized with the

Holy Spirit and endued with a new power from on high.

How the Church needs this power today! Without it the Church will never succeed in its mission to the world, despite all its grand organization and its vast material resources. With this power, not even the gates of hell can prevail against it.

Some years ago I was being guided through one of our new mission hospitals in India. When we came to the operating theatre, I noticed a great variety of surgical instruments neatly placed in the cupboard. One of these caught my eye in particular. It was a simple rod, with a triangular-shaped loop of platinum wire on one end and an electric cord attached to the other. I said to the doctor in charge, "What do you call this instrument?"

She answered, "That's what we call a cauterer. It is a very useful instrument in surgery. It can cut through the flesh with the greatest of ease." Seeing that I was rather puzzled by its appearance, she plugged the cord into a socket nearby, and suddenly the platinum wire began to glow with intense heat. "Now," she said, "If I were to place this on your arm, with the slightest pressure it would cut into your flesh immediately."

I saw an illustration in that instrument that day. Without the power of the Holy Spirit, we are like that cauterer, unplugged, and therefore ineffective. With the power of the Holy Spirit, we are like that instrument, "plugged in," glowing with heat, and ready for use. It's the Holy Spirit that makes the difference. He is able to bring hidden talents to the fore, to quicken natural abilities, and to sharpen our skills for effective service in His kingdom.

III. THE HOLY SPIRIT BURNS ON AND ON

One of the chief qualities of fire is its ability to light other fires. From a tiny spark a great blaze may result. A few years ago on the outskirts of Los Angeles someone threw a smoldering cigarette along the road.

It set fire to a few dry leaves, and they in turn set the trees on fire. Soon there was a tremendous conflagration that swept through the woods, consuming hundreds of acres of fine timber, and threatening many homes. It took scores of firemen and forest rangers and the equipment of several townships to quench the blaze. The financial loss was estimated in the millions of dollars. All on account of a tiny spark from a lighted cigarette!

The fire of the Holy Spirit has the ability to spread. It lights a flame on the altar of an individual, and through him it spreads to the members of his family. It lights a flame on the altar of a pastor's heart and through him sets fire to the whole congregation. It sparks the life of some layman, and through him starts a spiritual blaze in the whole community.

Many years ago the Holy Spirit lit a fire in the heart of a young Anglican minister in England, John Wesley by name, and through him it spread throughout the whole land of England, bringing spiritual revival and social revolution. Sometime after that the Holy Spirit lit a fire in the heart of a young British shoemaker, William Carey by name, and through him it spread to other members of the Church and even the clergy. This resulted in the inauguration of the modern era of Christian missions, perhaps the greatest period in the history of the Church. More recently the Holy Spirit lit a fire in the heart of a young, unknown, North Carolina boy, Billy Graham by name, and through him the flame spread all around the world, resulting in one of the greatest evagelistic thrusts in the history of the Christian Church.

Several years ago a downtown church in St. Paul, Minnesota, was destroyed by fire. Within the sanctuary of the church there was a marble replica of the Thorvaldsen's famous statue, "The Appealing Christ." It portrayed the Master standing with outstretched hands as if He were saying, "Come unto me, all ye that labour and are heavy laden, and I will give you rest." In some miraculous way the statue escaped injury in the fire and stood there amid the charred ruins in all its original beauty.

The next morning as people passed by on their way to work and surveyed the wreckage, their eyes fell upon the statue. The charred surroundings only seemed to enhance its beauty and appeal. Many took time to walk over close to the statue, and found themselves standing before it, gazing into the face of the loving Saviour, and spending a few moments in silent meditation. Soon people from all parts of the city came, and stepped through the ruins to get a closer view of the marble figure. The statue became the talk of the town.

The interesting part of this story is that the marble statue of Christ had been in the city of St. Paul for many years, but its existence and beauty were known to only a few worshipers who assembled in that church on Sunday morning. But when the church caught on fire, the whole city came to see it!

Too long Christ has been shut up within the four walls of the church, so that the outside world has not been conscious of His presence nor aware of His glory. But when the Church receives its baptism with the Holy Spirit and is set on fire, then all men will begin to see the Saviour. Instead of His message being confined to one man, the pastor, it will become the possession of every man in the pew. Instead of the message being restricted to a half-hour homiletical effort on Sunday morning, it will be heard in many a conversation throughout the week. Instead of the message being confined to the sanctuary of the church, it will be heard in home, factory, schoolroom, and office.

The story is told of a man in a certain community who never darkened the door of the church and proudly proclaimed himself to be an atheist. Though the local pastor tried his best, he could not get this individual to take an interest in the church. One day fire broke out in the church, and people came running from all directions to help put out the blaze. This was the day of the horse-drawn fire truck and the bucket brigade.

To his surprise, the pastor found the so-called atheist on the front line of the brigade, working strenuously to quench the flames. Jokingly the pastor said to him, "This is the first time I've seen you at church."

"Yes," quickly replied the atheist as he threw another bucket of water on the blaze, "and this is the first time I've ever seen your church on fire!"

When the Church of Jesus Christ receives its baptism with the fire of the Holy Spirit, it will be able to minister more effectively to the world, and the world will give greater attention to what it says and does.

The baptism by Christ with the Holy Spirit is not something secondary, but primary. It is not excess baggage, but essential equipment. It is not something we can take or leave as we desire; it is something we must have for effective living.

Dr. E. Stanley Jones, veteran missionary to India and evangelist to the world, testifies out of his long experience: "I came to India with this conviction and the years have done nothing but verify it. It is this—Pentecost is not a spiritual luxury; it is an utter necessity for human living. The human spirit fails unless the Holy Spirit fills. We are shut up to the alternative: Pentecost or failure."

In the state of California, in the summer months, a very magnificent spectacle is enacted daily amid the breathtaking beauty of Yosemite National Park. During the afternoon, on top of the cliff, a huge bed of coals is prepared. Just about dusk the spectators gather in the valley below.

Suddenly a voice from above pierces the stillness of the evening and echoes through the canyon: "Hello, Camp Curry. Are you ready?"

"Yes," comes the answer from below, "we are ready. Is the fire ready?"

"Yes, the fire is ready."

"Let the fire fall!"

And at that moment the huge bed of coals is pushed off the cliff, where they cascade a thousand feet down the precipice, in a never-to-be-forgotten fire-fall that leaves one speechless with its magnificence.

Goaded by our failure and weakness, as we look

upward imploringly, the voice of God pierces the stillness of our hearts, and we hear Him say, "Beloved, are you ready?"

With quickened heartbeat we answer back, "Yes, Lord, we are ready. Is the fire ready?"

Reassuringly comes the answer, "Yes, the fire is ready. It has been ready since the Day of Pentecost."

With waiting, expectant hearts we cry, "Let the fire fall!"

And at that moment God opens the windows of heaven and pours out His Spirit upon us, while refining fire goes through our souls, burning up the dross to produce purity; burning within to produce power; and burning on and on perpetually until many cold hearts have been warmed at the altars of our hearts. He is the God who answers by fire.

4

Purity in the Deep Mind

Be ye transformed by the renewing of your mind.
(Rom. 12:2)

*Have your mind renewed, and so be transformed in
nature* (Moffatt).

The great evangelist Dwight L. Moody once said,
"I have had more trouble with myself than with any
other man I ever met." Most of us in our moments
of utter honesty could, no doubt, make a similar confession.

This is due to our dual nature of dust and deity.
There is one part of us that honestly intends to be
clean and kind and truthful and forgiving; and there is
another part of us that is the source of thoughts
we ought not to have and dreams of which we are
ashamed, and prompts us to say things we are later
sorry for. Paul states the problem succinctly when he
says: "I do not understand my own actions. For I do
not do what I want, but I do the very thing I hate.
Now if I do what I do not want, I agree that the law
is good. So it is no longer I that do it, but sin which
dwells within me. For I know that nothing good dwells

within me, that is, in my flesh. I can will what is right, but I cannot do it. For I do not do the good I want, but the evil I do not want is what I do (Rom. 7:15-19, RSV).

It would seem that there are a good man and another not so good living in the same person, and the problem this fact poses is how to change the one who is not so desirable into the nature of the other.

Paul not only states the problem, but he also suggests the clue to its solution. "Be ye transformed," he writes, "by the renewing of your mind." The mind is the key to the man, and the way to become a completely transformed person is by the refashioning of the mind.

Before we look at the process of the renewal of the mind, let us seek first to understand some of the basic facts concerning the mind itself.

The first fact is that *the mind is a much more complex affair than we normally suppose.* Below the level of the consciousness there exists more of what we call mind. (It will come as welcome news to us that we have more mind than that of which we are conscious!) Thus we live in two minds: the conscious and the unconscious.

A part of our thinking process is occupied with the area of immediate awareness. In the focus of our attention are certain facts of which we are immediately aware. At present, for example, I am conscious of sitting at the typewriter writing these words; you are conscious of sitting in a chair or lying in bed, reading this book. But we know also there is another area of our minds that is occupied by thoughts that are not in the focus of attention, but that can be recalled at any moment we wish. If while we are sitting in church, the sermon loses interest for us, we can immediately retreat from the present into the past and begin to think of the good time we had on our last vacation, or on that last date, or on some holiday trip. Thus there are two areas: (1) that of immediate awareness, and (2), that of which we are entirely unconscious but which can be recalled at will.

We may compare the human mind to an iceberg. Seven-eighths of the bulk of the iceberg is below the level of the water. So with the mind. Only a fraction of it is above the level of consciousness; by far the larger part is buried down there below the surface in the unconscious.

Or we may compare the human mind to a factory with machinery turning over day and night, twenty-four hours a day. The mind is always at work, even while we are asleep. It takes the thoughts that we feed into it during our waking hours as raw material, and works on them all the time. We know this from personal experience. We can go to sleep having set our "mental alarm" to wake up at a certain hour, and we know what happens. That thought is uppermost in our sleeping mind, and wakes us up at all hours of the night. If we go to sleep with thoughts of anxiety and fear in our minds, we will be doubly fearful and anxious when we awaken. But if we go to sleep with thoughts of confidence and peace and the power of God to meet our needs, we will awaken with a deepened sense of adequacy and ability to meet our needs. That's why it is so valuable to have a prayer, or quote some Scripture, or think some noble, positive thoughts before dropping off to sleep.

So then we begin the attack on our problem by noticing that the mind is a complex affair by reason of the fact of its depth in the unconscious.

The second fact about the human mind that we must face is that *our lives are influenced by this deep mind as well as by this surface mind*—sometimes more.

David Seabury, noted psychologist, claims that three-fourths of our mental activity transpires below the level of our awareness, and comes to the surface only as the time of active use arrives. Dr. Charles Mayo says that 75 percent of human action is controlled by the unconscious, and only 25 percent by the conscious mind.

For example, take this actual case of a certain Sunday school teacher who became a "convinced atheist."

He claimed that he reached this position rationally by study and thought. Psychological analysis, however, revealed the real complex responsible for his atheism. The girl to whom he had been engaged eloped with the most enthusiastic of his fellow Sunday school teachers. Thus resentment against his successful rival had expressed itself by a repudiation of the beliefs which had formerly constituted the principal bond between them. The arguments were merely an elaborate rationalization.

Here is a young lad who lives most of the time alone with his mother. The father's duties as an evangelist or a salesman take him away from home for several weeks at a time. Normally the youngster is quite well-behaved when he is with his mother, but when the father comes home, he always "acts up." Deep down in the unconscious mind of the young lad is an inner resentment against his father for his long absences from home. So when Dad comes home, the boy "takes it out on him."

Sometimes deep-seated attitudes and emotions in the unconscious mind can throw sand into the human machinery and result in outer physical afflictions. Several years ago when I was pastor in a city in India, I was called to the home of a woman who had suddenly lost her eyesight and was receiving treatment from one of the local physicians. Previous to this she had never had any trouble with her eyes. When I called upon the doctor and inquired about the diagnosis, he said to me, "Reverend, there is really nothing organically wrong with this lady's eyes. This is the temporary result of some disturbing emotional experience. I am merely giving her superficial treatment to help psychologically. Perhaps you can discover the real reason for her trouble and offer her some more substantial help."

I went back to see the lady, and after much tactful probing and a time of prayer together, the truth finally came out. Within the past few days she had suddenly discovered that her husband was unfaithful. She thought she had lost his love and therefore lost him. The sudden case of blindness was an unconscious attempt on her part to win back his affection and his attention. Now he would have to give much of his time to her, and actually lead her about by the hand.

When I went to see the husband and placed the whole matter before him, he came to his senses and repented of his wrongdoing. He asked his wife for forgiveness, and the two were wonderfully reconciled. In a day or two the lady's eyesight was completely restored!

So it is that many of the things we do, entirely unknown to ourselves, are governed by the deep mind down below the level of consciousness.

The third fact about the human mind that we must face is that elements in *this deep mind are by nature inclined to evil.*

It is in that part of our minds below the level of consciousness that we get human nature in the raw. It is there that the instincts, like sex and the ego, reign supreme. These instincts have come down through a long line of racial history. They drive for completion. It is from the depths of the unconscious mind that some of our dreams arise, and it is out of that abyss that our impure thoughts are born. And there we have the reason why so often we find the good life so difficult to achieve.

In conversion, a new love and loyalty are introduced. Jesus is accepted into the conscious mind as Lord and Saviour. But the unconscious mind often doesn't accept that. The driving urges sometimes go against the morality built up in the conscious mind. So while the conscious mind is civilized, the deep mind is still partially savage. The conscious mind is Christian, but the deep mind is somewhat pagan. The conscious mind has been converted, but the deep mind is still not fully aligned with the will of God.

As a result we have a major conflict going on within ourselves. Down deep within us we feel tempers, lusts, and fears that have not been cleansed away. We feel like we are sitting on top of a volcano. Something down below pushes up. We are like a ship whose starboard turbines are pushing forward with its port engines backing up. One part of us says, "Get thee behind me, Satan," and another part says, "Get back there and push me on."

Now we see what the apostle means when he says, "I find then a law, that, when I would do good, evil is present with me. For I delight in the law of God after the inward man: but I see another law in my members, warring against the law of my mind, and bringing me into captivity to the law of sin which is in my members" (Rom. 7:21-23).

Can Christ redeem only the conscious mind? Is this the best He can do? Or can He also redeem the unconscious mind? Can He cleanse the depths? Or do we have to sit on the lid all the time?

I believe that the unconscious mind can be cleansed. Otherwise God has not made a full remedy for our malady. He has done only a half job.

After his vivid description of the inner conflict in the human mind, the Apostle Paul cries out in despair, "O wretched man that I am! who shall deliver me from the body of this death?" And immediately, in faith, he gives the answer to his own question, "I thank God through Jesus Christ our Lord" (Rom. 7:24-25).

And so we come to the point of the matter—the redemption of the deep mind. That means that in order to become fully transformed persons we, in a sense, require two conversions. There is first the conversion of the conscious mind, and that takes place when we initially come to Christ in repentance and decide we are going to follow Him. But more than that, we will never be delivered from inner conflict and find supreme joy in the Christian life until we go on to that second "conversion," the conversion of the deep mind. And this, I believe, is what the apostle means when he says, "Have your mind renewed, and so be transformed in nature" (Moffatt).

How can that be done? Let me suggest a few simple steps.

First, *recognize your inner impurity and conflict.*

Accept yourself as you are. Honestly and sincerely face up to your condition. Don't try to hide your inner feelings or rationalize concerning them, but clearly recognize their presence, and confess your need.

When Isaiah had a vision of God in all His holiness, then he had a vision of himself in all his impurity. In despair, he cried out, "Woe is me! for I am undone; because I am a man of unclean lips, and I dwell in the midst of a people of unclean lips" (Isa. 6:5).

The prophet Jeremiah, recognizing the sinful depths of the human heart, wrote from personal experience, "The heart is deceitful above all things, and desperately wicked: who can know it?" (Jer. 17:9).

When King David was rebuked by the prophet Nathan, he was convicted of his inner depravity as well as his outer transgressions, and cried out in true confession, "My sin is ever before me. Behold, I was shapen in iniquity; and in sin did my mother conceive me. Behold, thou desirest truth in the inward parts" (Ps. 51:3, 5-6).

On the occasion of one of his first encounters with Jesus, Simon Peter cried out, "Depart from me; for I am a sinful man, O Lord" (Luke 5:8).

The Apostle Paul, describing the inner conflict of his former life, wrote, "If I do what I do not want, it is no longer I that do it, but sin which dwells in me" (Rom. 7:20, RSV).

So the first step is to recognize your inner uncleanness and confess it to God.

Second, *have faith to believe that the Holy Spirit is able to reach down and work in depths that are beyond your control.*

It is comforting to realize that God is working directly upon the part of us that we cannot reach or control. The Sanctifier is there; the Spirit of Truth is there; the Healer is there—way down at the center of the disease, at the very heart of the problem. It is comforting to know that God ministers to the whole of us, to our consciousness and freedom, and also to our unconsciousness. The Spirit can heal and cleanse where our ideas and choices cannot penetrate fast enough. It is here that we most need the Spirit. The heart is bad. It needs to be remade through and through. And it is here that the Spirit perfects His work, making us Christlike.

Let your faith be based on the finished work of Christ and upon the direct promises of the Word of God. Paul states clearly that "Christ also loved the church, and gave himself for it; that he might sanctify and cleanse it with the washing of water by the word" (Eph. 5:25-26). In another place he writes, "He saved us not because of deeds done by us in righteousness, but in virtue of his own mercy, by the washing of regeneration and renewal in the Holy Spirit, which he poured out upon us richly through Jesus Christ our Savior" (Titus 3:5-6, RSV). And again, "We are sanctified through the offering of the body of Jesus Christ once for all" (Heb. 10:10).

God's promises concerning inner cleansing are also clear and specific. "How much more shall the blood of Christ, who through the eternal Spirit offered himself without spot [blemish] to God, purge your conscience from dead works to serve the living God?" (Heb. 9:14). "But if we walk in the light, as he is in the light, we have fellowship one with another, and the blood of Jesus Christ his Son cleanseth us from all sin" (I John 1:7).

Christ died to cleanse the depths. God in His Word promises to cleanse. The Holy Spirit stands ready to complete the work. Now exercise your faith and believe that He is able and willing to cleanse you—*now!*

Third, *pray a definite prayer to the Holy Spirit for your personal cleansing.*

Confess your inner impurity to Him. Call each thing by its true name. If it's lust, say so. If it's selfishness, say so. If it's resentment or hatred, say so. Now you are not confessing merely outward transgressions, but an inward condition. Say to the Spirit: "Lord, You know that down in my heart there are all kinds of things not pleasing to You—pride, jealousy, hatred, lust, selfishness, etc. I can't do anything about these things, so You'll have to help me. I don't seem to be able to control my inner mind, so You'll have to take control. Cleanse the very depths of my mind and heart, and take complete control of my innermost being—my motives, desires, ambitions, urges, instincts."

As you pray, believe. Say to yourself, He has offered; I have asked. He has promised; I do now receive. Say to the Spirit, "I do believe You cleanse me here and now. Thank You, Lord!" And let your faith rest peacefully on the promises of God, not on your feelings. Faith is simply accepting the statements of God as true, and true for *you*.

Fourth, *maintain an attitude of surrender and obedience.*

Remember, this is just the beginning. It is a *crisis* that initiates a *process*. This initial prayer must be followed by a daily attitude. The will must remain surrendered. The moment it begins to usurp authority from the Holy Spirit, the moment it says to itself, I'm going to run things, then at that moment the Holy Spirit is obstructed in His work of cleansing. The driving urges get out of control once again and the inner conflict emerges. As we surrender afresh daily, as we keep our wills on His side, the Holy Spirit keeps cleansing from moment to moment of each day. We must be sensitive to His guidance and checks; we must walk in the light; we must be obedient to His will.

If we take these definite steps, the Holy Spirit will move in and purify our driving urges at depths we cannot control. He cleanses and consecrates them.

He cleanses the ego or self-urge from selfishness, and dedicates it to the kingdom of God. Self is still there, because it is still a part of us. We can't be *selfless* men, but we can be *unselfish* men. If we were selfless, we would not be men. Our Lord was not selfless. He made a tremendous impact upon the world with Himself. But most certainly He was unselfish. The self was organized around God.

We can't get rid of the driving urges. They are a part of our essential humanity. We can't get rid of self. We try to put it out the front door, and it comes back through the window, often dressed in a religious garb. The question is: Who's got the self? Has self got itself and therefore is it building life around itself? Or has the Holy Spirit got it?

The Holy Spirit cleanses the sex urge from sensuality and dedicates it for God-given purposes—procreation and love, within the bonds of marriage. When sex and human love are sanctified by the power of the Holy Spirit and are under His control, they become a powerful instrument for the good and stability of the home. When sex and love get out of His control, they can become a powerful force for evil and destruction of virtue.

Suppose a man is unmarried, then what? Is he always frustrated? No. The sex urge is the creative urge. It can create physically in the home or spiritually outside the home. In the hands of God, it can be sublimated to produce new movements and new people. So the unmarried person can express the creative urge on *another* (note, not a *higher*) level, ministering to other people as a loving parent, creating new ideas. Then he is not frustrated, but integrated.

The sex urge is still there. We can't wipe it out. It's a good thing, a driving force. We need to surrender it to God. Then He controls it and creates through it. If we try to suppress it, we have complexes and neuroses. But if we surrender it, we have freedom.

Then also, *the Holy Spirit cleanses and controls the social urge*. This is the urge within us that seeks the company of other people, that seeks the approval and favor of society. People outside Christ will fasten this urge onto other people, the world, and society. Those in Christ will fasten this urge onto the kingdom of God, the fellowship of His people. That's the society to which we must be loyal. Then we are no longer just echoes, but voices; not just robots, but people.

It is interesting that the Apostle Paul immediately precedes the words of the text, "Be ye transformed by the renewing of your mind," with the admonition, "Be not conformed to the world" (Rom. 12:2). J. B. Phillips in his modern English translation puts the complete verse in these graphic words: "Don't let the world around you squeeze you into its own mould, but let God re-mould your minds from within." Paul realized that the only antidote to keep the social urge from becoming a slave to the whims and fashions of society, was for it to be under the control of the Holy Spirit, who dwells within the believer.

All these urges—self, sex, and the social urge must be both *cleansed* and *consecrated*. If only cleansed, then there would still be danger. They must be consecrated to their God-given purposes. The cleansing is negative; the consecration is positive.

We must be willing to be cleansed and consecrated. Then the Holy Spirit has charge of our driving urges and controls them, with our consent and cooperation. Therefore there is no struggle. We're not fighting all the time. We are surrendering and trusting. This makes us relaxed and released.

So the unconscious can be remade, and then it will remake us. Jesus said, "The good man brings good out of his good store, and the evil man brings evil out of his store of evil" (Matt. 12:35, Moffatt). He thus pictures the deep mind as a bank. We can't draw out of a bank something we have not first put in. Every time we make a deposit of a good thought, a good deed, a good attitude, we build up our balance in the good store; and the "good store" is the factory that in the deep mind works even while we sleep, and begins to transform the nature.

It is possible to build up a good store from day to day. Then when a crisis comes our way, these inner resources throw themselves into the battle and help us on to victory. We become safer and safer as we walk the Christian way. We more or less naturally do the right thing. Thus the deep mind, that left to itself is a terrible drag on the good life, can actually be made to work in our favor. Instead of being an enemy, it becomes an *ally*.

The opposite is also possible. We can build up an evil store. Every evil thought (if nurtured) or wrong attitude doesn't just pass through the conscious mind, but goes down into the unconscious mind and lodges there. If one is jealous, lustful, or resentful, it drops down into the deep mind and leaves a deposit. Then when temptation or some crisis comes, it pushes itself upward into the conscious mind and emerges in an outward action. When a seemingly good man goes wrong, we say, "How could he do it?" The reason is that it was down below all the time and just came to the surface.

The Holy Spirit works clear down in the unconscious mind, cleansing, consecrating, and controlling our inner desires, motives, feelings, and attitudes. He helps us to build up a good store and thus establishes us in the Christian life. All of this takes place, of course, as long as we surrender, cooperate, and obey.

Redemption thus goes clear to the depths. Christ can redeem the unconscious as well as the conscious mind.

God promises: "Then will I sprinkle clean water upon you, and ye shall be clean: from all your filthiness, and from all your idols, will I cleanse you. A new heart also will I give you, and a new spirit will I put within you: and I will also take away the stony heart out of your flesh, and I will give you an heart of flesh. And I will put my spirit within you, and cause you to walk in my statutes, and ye shall keep my judgments, and to them" (Ezek. 36:25-27).

John, the beloved disciple, reiterates the promise: "If we walk in the light, as he is in the light . . . the blood of Jesus Christ His Son cleanseth us from all sin" (I John 1:7).

Pray the prayer of David from the depths of your heart: "Wash me thoroughly from mine iniquity, and cleanse me from my sin. Create in me a clean heart, O God; and renew a right spirit within me" (Ps. 51: 2, 10).

Remembering the physical leper who came to Jesus one day asking for help, come to Him now as a spiritual leper, using the same words of confidence—"If you want to, you can make me clean" (Matt. 8:2, Phillips). Then hear Him speak the word of healing: "Of course I want to. Be clean!"

66

5

Power in the Inner Man

And, behold, I send the promise of my Father upon you: but tarry ye in the city of Jerusalem, until ye be endued with power from on high (Luke 24:49).

You shall receive power when the Holy Spirit has come upon you; and you shall be my witness in Jerusalem and in all Judea and Samaria and to the end of the earth (Acts 1:8, RSV).

The prepositional phrases our Lord uses in His promises concerning the Holy Spirit make an interesting study. He says, "I will send him unto you" (John 16:7); again, "He shall be in you" (John 14:17); then again, "After that the Holy Ghost is come upon you" (Acts 1:8); and finally, "Out of his heart shall flow rivers of living water" (John 7:38, RSV). Note: "Unto you," "in you," "upon you," and "out of [you]."

Each preposition is important. "Unto you" declares the sending of the Holy Spirit by Christ Himself—His Gift to us. "In you" indicates the indwelling presence of the Holy Spirit—His cleansing work. "Out of you" symbolizes the outflow of the Holy Spirit in rich blessings to others. "Upon you" signifies the baptism with the Holy Spirit—the enduement with power from on high. In this meditation we shall consider the last truth —the relationship of the Holy Spirit to spiritual power.

It is significant that in the two instances in which Jesus used the phrase "upon you," He linked the coming of the Holy Spirit with power. Jesus spoke of the Spirit as "the Comforter," and probably the best translation of the word is "Strengthener"—*con* meaning "with," and *fortis* meaning "strength." Thus the Holy Spirit is the One who strengthens us by being with us. When He is within us, then we are unified, and hence fortified. We go places; we do things.

THE CHARACTERISTICS OF THIS POWER

There are three distinct characteristics of this power that is made available to us through the indwelling presence of the Holy Spirit.

First, *it is power "from on high."* Note the words "until ye be endued with power from on high." In other words, this is a power *outside of ourselves.*

There are two approaches to this matter of finding spiritual power. One is the approach of developing power within ourselves. The other is to receive it from without. The first is the method of self-realization or self-improvement. It admonishes us: "Awaken your hidden resources"; "Cultivate your inner powers." But the benefit of this procedure is limited. Since it begins with the self, it ends with the resources of the self. It's like the young aspiring "Atlas" who goes through his daily routine of calisthenics, lifting his barbells and pulling on the stretch bands. He can develop his muscles to a certain extent, no doubt, but he can develop them only so far.

But the power that Jesus is talking about is not from within, but from on high. It is not attained, but *obtained;* not developed, but *received.* It is not the result of our own efforts; it is a *gift.* Therefore it is unlimited! It is resources from God to man.

Some would argue that only the morally weak seek power outside of themselves; the strong can rely on their own strength. But this is not the way people reason or act in the physical realm. They are constantly looking for new sources of physical and mechanical power; and are most eager to avail themselves of these sources.

For example, there are two ways to cross the continent. I may start out on foot, and after days and days of walking, finally make it. Or I can take a jet plane and make the journey in a few hours. There are two ways to cross the ocean. I may strike out swimming (and never make it), or I can avail myself of the power of steam and turbine and cross the seas comfortably and safely in a modern ocean liner. There are two ways to dig the foundation for a building. I may use pickaxe and shovel, and after weeks of toil and sweat finally complete the job, or I can use one of those giant bulldozers and complete the task quickly and efficiently.

When great spiritual resources outside of ourselves are at our disposal, why do we want to go on in the weak and limited strength of human self-sufficiency? When temptation comes, we can either face it in our own strength, and doubtless fall a prey to the enemy, or we can resist in the power of the Spirit and cause the tempter to flee. When trials and burdens overwhelm like a flood, we can grit our teeth and clench our fists and say, "I must grin and bear it," and probably be crushed under the weight of it all; or we can call on God's grace and strength, use the trials for His glory and our own good, and come out victorious and better Christians.

You can take your choice. You can say if you like, "I want to be independent. I want to use my own powers," and head out across country on foot. (I'll take the jet, thank you.) You can start swimming across the Atlantic. (I'll take the *Queen Elizabeth,* if you don't mind.) Or you can start digging your hole by hand. (I'll take a bulldozer any day.) If you so desire, you can face life in your own strength and try to overcome temptation and trials in your own weakness; but as for me, I'll take the grace of God and call on

His mighty resources and power. I prefer power "from on high."

In the second place, *this is power "in the inner man."* The Apostle Paul prays for the Christians at Ephesus that they might "be strengthened with might by his Spirit in the inner man" (Eph. 3:16). A few verses further on, he describes this power as "the power at work *within us*" (20, RSV).

It is the inner man that makes the outer man. If the inner life is weak, then weakness spreads to the outer life. If there is confusion within, there will be confusion without. The Holy Spirit is Power where it counts—in the inner man. The Spirit doesn't give us a shot in the arm that lifts temporarily and then lets us slump. He strengthens us with might in the very fiber of our being.

The difference in a person before and after the in-filling of the Holy Spirit is the difference between a sailboat and a steamboat. The sailboat depends on environment, or circumstances. When the wind blows, it sails ahead; when the wind ceases, it stops. The steamboat depends on "inner-stances"; it has power within and goes ahead with or without the help of the wind. Some are sailboat Christians—they are *circumstance-driven*. Others are steamboat Christians—they are *Spirit-driven*. We are not to be *self-sufficient* but *Spirit-sufficient*.

Bishop Brenton T. Bradley, former leader of the Methodist church in India, used to tell a humorous parable about a missionary and his Model A Ford. One day while the missionary was touring in the villages, one of the tires suddenly went flat. Not having a spare tire along with him, or any equipment to repair the puncture, he was at a loss to know what to do. But then he noticed some bundles of straw that had dropped along the side of the road from a passing bullock cart. So he removed the tube, stuffed the tire with straw, and proceeded on his way. This seemed to work satisfactorily enough, so that the missionary never bothered to have the tube repaired. In the course of time the other three tires had punctures, and the missionary followed the same procedure. Then one day the engine itself developed trouble and the car came to a standstill. The missionary walked to the nearest village, hired a couple of strong bullocks, hitched them up to the front, and had the car pulled the rest of the way.

The missionary thought to himself, Well, why not just keep the bullocks and let them pull the car wherever I go? It will save the cost of repairing the engine and also buying gasoline. So he ended up with straw in all the tires and a pair of bullocks up front!

Then the good bishop would make his point. "Many Christians are like that. Having no resources or power within, they rely on being pulled about here and there by some secondary outside forces. God wants to put His Spirit and His power within us. That's where it counts the most."

On one occasion I used this parable in a sermon to a group of Christian workers and Bible students in south India. When I had finished, a young Indian evangelist jumped to his feet and said, "Brother Seamands, I have a confession to make. I am just like the missionary you told about in that story. I have been full of dead straw, not the life-giving breath of the Spirit. I want all of you to pray with me that I might be filled with the Spirit and strengthened with power in the inner man." Recent reports on the ministry of this revitalized young man indicate that his preaching is making a tremendous impact upon the people wherever he goes.

In the third place, *this power from on high is strictly spiritual power*. Since it is the power of the Spirit, it is therefore spiritual in nature.

Up to Pentecost the disciples believed in the spirit of retaliation, in the use of physical force to gain spiritual ends. We readily recall several instances in which this was true. James and John wanted to call down fire from heaven on the Samaritans. On the night of the Crucifixion, Peter sought to defend his Master with a sword. Even on the last day that Jesus was with His disciples, they expected the kingdom of Israel to be restored.

But after Pentecost they relied on spiritual weapons—the power of love and faith and forgiveness. They overcame evil with good, hate with love, the world by a cross. They believed that mercy was stronger than might, love was stronger than law, forgiveness was stronger than force, faith was stronger than fear. When Peter spoke to the crowd in Jerusalem on the Day of Pentecost, he addressed them as "brethren" (see Acts 2:29). When Stephen was being stoned by the mob in Jerusalem, he cried out with a loud voice, "Lord, lay not this sin to their charge" (Acts 7:60). When Ananias was sent by God to call on the new convert Saul, as he prayed in a certain home, he called this dreaded enemy of the church "brother" (Acts 9:17). This was the spirit that enabled them to overcome the world. And this is the spirit that will help us to overcome today.

A young British soldier knelt by his bedside in prayer one night at the barracks. A half-drunken, cursing "Tommy" mocked his piety and flung his heavy, muddy boots at the kneeling form. The Christian boy never said a word, but finished his prayer and crawled into bed. In the morning the soldier who had struck at the Christian found his boots cleaned and polished and neatly placed by his bed. When he discovered who had done the job, his heart melted in repentance, and he came to the young man for forgiveness and spiritual help. What might could not do, love accomplished in silence.

Several years ago in one of the villages of south India, a farmer was won to Christ through the witness of a YMCA secretary. The man was baptized and joined the church. His old friends turned against him, set fire to his crops, and even chopped off one of his hands. Some of the more sensitive residents in the village said among themselves, "This is gross injustice. Those men ought to be punished."

So they collected funds for the new convert to hire a lawyer and take legal action against his enemies. But when the YMCA secretary brought the money to the farmer, the latter quietly refused the money, saying, "Sir, I am a lowly villager. You are a learned man. When you were instructing me in the Christian faith, you taught me that Jesus prayed on the Cross for His enemies, 'Father, forgive them; for they know not what they do.' If I am to follow Christ, I must also forgive my enemies. They too didn't know what they were doing. I'm sorry, I can't accept the money. I can't go to court."

As a result of this witness, the whole community was shaken to the depths. Several accepted Christ and joined the church. What law could not do, love graciously accomplished.

Such spiritual power comes to the human spirit only through the inner working of the Holy Spirit. He not only redeems us from wrong *actions*, but wrong *reactions* as well. He not only transforms our outer deportment, but also our inner dispositions.

This is "power from on high," "power in the inner man," and a power that is spiritual in nature.

THE OBJECTIVES OF THIS POWER

The power of the Holy Spirit is made available to us for two distinct purposes: to enable us to (1) face life victoriously, and (2) witness effectively.

To Face Life Victoriously

Notice that Jesus instructed His disciples to "tarry in the city." One would think it would have been better for them to retire, say, to some mountain in Galilee, and there in the solitude to wait upon God. But there was a reason for this command. The city is the place of congested populations and concentrated problems. It is the place of complex relationships and conflicting responsibilities. It is the place of storm and stress, of tension and temptations. In such a place as this they were to tarry. Jesus was trying to show them that the power of the Holy Spirit is adequate for the toughest, most adverse environment. No situation, no problem is too hard for the Spirit. And if He can keep us victorious in the big city, with all its problems and tensions, then He can keep us victorious anywhere else.

Jesus also specified that the disciples were to tarry "in the city of Jerusalem." Why not in Jericho or Capernaum or Nazareth? In the first place, Jerusalem was the scene of the Crucifixion. It was there that the Master had been tried, scourged, crucified, and buried. It was there that He suffered what was apparently His greatest defeat. But Jesus wanted to demonstrate to His disciples that, through the Holy Spirit, He would turn the place of the greatest tragedy into the place of the greatest triumph. In the very city where He had been crucified He would build His Church. In the very place where He had been rejected shamefully He would reign supreme. And if He was victorious in Jerusalem, He would be victorious everywhere else.

Furthermore, Jerusalem was the place of defeat for the disciples. It was there that they had fled and hid themselves behind closed doors. It was there that Peter had denied his Lord three times. Jerusalem was the place of shame and sorrow, of defeat and discouragement. But Jesus wanted to demonstrate to His disciples that the place of their greatest defeat would become the place of their greatest victory. Where they had denied their Master, they would now declare Him to be Lord. Where they had once feared the minority, they would now face the multitudes. Where they had once scattered like sheep, they would now gather the lost sheep into the Father's fold. And if they could be triumphant in Jerusalem, then victory would be theirs wherever they went.

In my second term of missionary service in India, I was appointed superintendent of one of the southern districts. In youthful confidence and enthusiasm, I began the term with a burst of evangelistic zeal. But soon I found myself bogged down with administrative responsibilities and entangled in complex problems.

In one of the quarterly conference sessions a rather selfish and carnally minded layman, who had hoped to be elected as delegate to annual conference and had electioneered with great zeal for the position, was soundly defeated in the election by a more worthy candidate. He stalked out of the meeting in a fit of anger, striking at one of the senior Indian ministers on his way out. In a few days I received a summons from the local court, giving me notice of a civil case that this brother had brought against me and the officers of the quarterly conference. His plea was that the business meeting was contrary to the church rules of order, and therefore the election should be declared null and void. Naturally I felt very hurt and ashamed to be involved in a court case with a fellow church member.

Not long afterward I received a second summons from the court. On account of the lack of funds, I had released one of the temporary office workers from mission employment. He took the matter to court, demanding all sort of financial compensation.

When I received the second summons, my heart sank to the depths of despondency. Almost in tears I said to my wife, "Well, Honey, I've had enough. It's time for us to pack up and go back home to the States. I came to India to preach the gospel, not to go to court—and against my own Christian brethren at that. I'm going to send in my letter of resignation."

My wife felt the pain of the whole affair along with me, but she wisely advised me to be patient and take the matter to the Lord in prayer.

I went into my office, shut the door, and began to pour out my heart to the Lord. Suddenly it seemed as if a voice spoke within me: "You're trying to run away from your problems, aren't you? This isn't the way out. Tarry in the city of Jerusalem until you be endued with power from on high. Belgaum is your Jerusalem. Stay at your post of duty; surrender yourself and the whole problem into My hands; and I will turn the place of defeat into the place of victory."

Through my tears I confessed the bitterness that had crept into my heart and the carnal means that I was beginning to use in the struggle against my brethren. I surrendered myself anew to the Lord and asked Him to fill me afresh with the Holy Spirit and His love.

I cannot describe in detail all that followed. It suffices to say that the battle was not won in the courts but in my heart. Slowly but surely the problems began to dissolve. The first man became ashamed of himself and withdrew the case from court. The second man pursued his case, but it was settled with minor adjustments. But this is only part of the story. The other part is more thrilling and significant. When the heart of the missionary was renewed, revival came to the central church in the city and then spread to the whole district. The Christians were spiritually revived and strengthened, while many non-Christians in the outlying villages were brought to the feet of the Saviour. Business sessions in the rural quarterly conferences gave way to spontaneous preaching and altar invitations and glowing testimonies of victory. As the Spirit came upon both missionary and nationals, the place of shameful defeat was literally turned into the place of glorious victory; the place of weakness became the place of power. In addition, a spirit of contagious joy permeated the Christian community in all its activities and relationships. The joy of the Lord became our strength.

The power of the Holy Spirit is given to us to enable us to be victorious and radiant in our personal lives.

To witness effectively

Between the twentieth chapter of John's Gospel and the second chapter of the Book of Acts we are presented with three different pictures of the disciples.

First, we find them *behind closed doors.* In John 20:19 we read that "the doors were shut where the disciples were assembled for fear of the Jews." A few verses farther on we read: "And after eight days again his disciples were within, . . . the doors being shut" (v. 26). Ringing in their ears were the most gracious words that had ever been spoken—the message of Jesus. They had seen the most perfect exhibition of living the world has ever known—His life. They had witnessed earth's most terrific and decisive moral struggle—His crucifixion. They had been eyewitnesses of the most astonishing fact in history—His resurrection. They had seen wounds that would heal all wounds, a death that would banish all death, a resurrection that would raise the world into new life. They had received the command to go share this news with the whole world. Yet, with all of this back of them, what had they done? They had shut themselves up behind closed doors for fear of the people. They had the message the world needed, the only message that could cure the sin-hurt of the world, and yet that message was shut behind closed doors.

In the next scene, we see the disciples *on their knees*. In the opening verses of Acts we read: "And when they were come in, they went up into an upper room. . . . These all continued with one accord in prayer and supplication" (Acts 1:13-14).

The crisis made them desperate; it sent them to the place of prayer. When a man is down, the best thing he can do is fall on his knees—not lie on his back. When a man falls on his knees, he'll soon be on his feet again. Note, they didn't hold a conference, or form a new committee, or put on a new drive. They held a prayer meeting, formed a new partnership with God, and arose with new determination in their hearts. "When the day of Pentecost was fully come . . . they were all filled with the Holy Ghost, and began to speak with other tongues, as the Spirit gave them utterance" (Acts 2:1-4).

In the third scene, we find the disciples *out in the open*. They threw open the doors of the upper room, stepped out on the balcony, and fearlessly declared to the multitude assembled in the street below that Jesus was "Lord and Christ," the "Prince of Life." Gone were hesitancy and fear. These had given way to certainty and courage. The disciples were now on the march. Nothing could stop them—no, not even threatening, scourging, or imprisonment! Filled with the Holy Spirit, they filled all Jerusalem with their message. (Compare Acts 2:4 and 5:28.)

The only power that could get the disciples out

from behind closed doors and loose them and their message upon the world was the power of the Holy Spirit. Christ's message, His life, His commission, even His resurrection, were not enough. Only Pentecost got them out. For up to Pentecost the whole thing was on the outside of them—now it was within.

The Church in general today is in many respects a Church behind closed doors. We have the Word of God; we have the commission; we have the machinery and the resources—but we have no power and no witness. We are hiding behind closed *doors of fear*. The forces of secularism, materialism, and agnosticism press in from all directions within the country itself. From without there is the power of atheistic Communism, that threatens to engulf the world and strikes fear in the heart of every man.

We are hiding behind closed *doors of doubt*. We have lost our convictions concerning the inspiration and authenticity of the sacred Scriptures. The concepts of relativism and universalism have dulled the sharp edge of our evangelistic fervor and our missionary motivation. We are not sure anymore that we have a message or a Saviour who is unique. We are not certain whether we have a right to call others out of their religion into faith in Jesus Christ and Him alone.

We are hiding behind *doors of worldliness*. We have lost our moral standards and our ethical integrity. Guilt lurks, jealousy festers, resentments consume, and impotency hangs about our necks. We have become so much like the outside world that we have little to offer that is different.

The crisis should make us desperate and send us to our knees. We need to find an upper room somewhere, where we can honestly search our hearts, make a new commitment and surrender to Christ, and receive the fulness of the Holy Spirit, which will send us out to face the world and all its moral sickness and degradation with new confidence, courage, and power. And we must face it with a contagious joy. It's not more men or money we need, but more of the Spirit of Christ.

What if the early disciples had not tarried? Suppose for a moment there had been no Pentecost. The upper room would have become their tomb. They would have died spiritually. The Church never would have been born.

What if we don't tarry today? Then there is no hope for the future. We're here today because the early Christians tarried, because men and women have tarried down through the centuries. The Church will exist tomorrow because we are tarrying today.

The Holy Spirit endues us with power from on high to make us effective witnesses to the grace and transforming power of the Lord Jesus Christ. He gives us boldness and strength to announce the good tidings of salvation, by conversation, exhortation, instruction, and testimony. Whether the individual be the preacher in the pulpit, or the leader in his class, or the teacher in the Sunday school, or the brother giving his testimony, or the friend conversing with friend, or the saint leading in prayer, the Holy Spirit imparts an unction to his words which not only gives him a gracious influence but a gracious power as well. They convict, awaken, inspire, transform. It is this heralding of the good tidings, this preaching of the gospel, not only by the ordained ministry but by the people of God generally, under the power of the Holy Spirit, that will usher in the kingdom of God—not the proclaiming of truth alone, but the heralding of truth with power sent from above.

The Steps to Power

I wish to suggest three words which will help us in this search for power and victory: Realize—Release —Receive!

Realize: We must first realize, or recognize, that there are vast spiritual resources at our disposal. We must realize that God is really what He claims to be; that He is all-powerful, all-wise, and a loving Heavenly Father. We need a vision of the greatness of God, His majesty and dominion and power. In his thought-provoking book *Your God Is Too Small,* J. B. Phillips contends that we have whittled down the size of our God. We have minimized Him, humanized Him, and dethroned Him. He suggests that we must quit thinking small and start thinking big about our God.

Furthermore, we must realize that these resources can really become a personal possession. They are ours for the asking. Electric power was always in the world. So was atomic power. Man only needed to discover them. Likewise, the power of God has always been in the world. We need only to discover it, to realize it.

Release: When scientists discovered the secret of the power of the atom, they realized that here was a source of tremendous power, but they had to discover ways and means of releasing that power. The power is there, but how to get it out? Look at an ordinary lump of uranium ore, for example, and you will see nothing but that. Yet when a scientist takes that lump of ore into his laboratory, he releases sufficient energy to shake the world. One scientist took an ordinary cardboard railway ticket from his pocket and said to a friend, "There is enough energy in that to drive an express train 10,000 miles." Then he added, "We will tackle sand next, just ordinary sand; and in two handfuls of sand there is enough energy to supply all the basic power of the U.S.A. for the next two to three years." The secret of atomic power lies in the principle of released energy.

How can we release the power of God in our lives, in situations? First, by *prayer.* One man said, "When I pray, I feel as if I am plugging in on the power of the universe." The Book of Acts gives us many illustrations of this truth. For example, "these all continued with one accord in prayer and supplication. . . . And when the day of Pentecost was fully come . . . they were all filled with the Holy Ghost" (1:14; 2:1, 4). When the disciples prayed, the Holy Spirit came upon them. "And at Midnight Paul and Silas prayed. . . . And suddenly there was a great earthquake, so that the foundations of the prison were shaken: and immediately all the doors were opened, and every one's bands were loosed" (16:25-26). Prayer shakes the foundations of lives and situations; it opens doors to service; it looses chains of bondage. "And when they had prayed, the place was shaken where they were assembled together; and they were all filled with the Holy Ghost, and they spake the word of God with boldness" (4:31). Prayer gives power to preach and to witness.

Again the power of God can be released through *faith*. Jesus said, "If ye have faith as a grain of mustard seed, ye shall say unto this mountain, Remove hence to yonder place; and it shall remove; and nothing shall be impossible unto you" (Matt. 17:20). Read the eleventh chapter of the Epistle to the Hebrews for the confirmation of these words of Jesus: "Through faith [they] subdued kingdoms, wrought righteousness, obtained promises, stopped the mouths of lions, quenched the violence of fire, escaped the edge of the sword, out of weakness were made strong, waxed valiant in fight, turned to flight the armies of the aliens. Women received their dead raised to life again" (Heb. 11:33-35).

It's not a great faith we need so much as a small faith in a great God. Unbelief blocks the flow of the power of God. Faith opens the floodgates and turns it loose.

Third, the power of God can be released through *surrender*. The Holy Spirit is within the believer; He is the Spirit of power. But we must not allow any blocks or hindrances to the power of God flowing through us. On an electric power line, if any place of resistance occurs, the wire will heat up and there will be a resultant power loss. As long as the line is clear, the power will flow.

Dwight L. Moody once heard someone say, "The world has yet to see what God can do with one who is completely surrendered to His will." Moody said, "I will be that man." No wonder his ministry was so effective! In one city the ministerial committee was discussing the possibility of inviting him back for a third city-wide campaign. One of the members objected and asked, "Why do you always want Dwight L. Moody? Does he have a monopoly on the Holy Spirit?"

Another quickly replied, "No, but the Holy Spirit has a monopoly on Dwight L. Moody!" Therein lies the secret.

Receive: Jesus said to His disciples, "Ye shall *receive* power, after that the Holy Ghost is come upon you" (Acts 1:8). Since this is a power from on high, apart from the resources of man, it cannot be developed or achieved. It can only be received. And how do we receive? Jesus said, "Ask, and it shall be given you. . . . For every one that asketh receiveth" (Luke 11: 9-10). It is as simple as that. Ask and receive.

But we must be careful about our motive in asking for this spiritual power. We must not seek power for itself. Power does not come as a separate entity. It is the result of an intimate relationship with the person of the Holy Spirit. Receive *Him,* and you've got *it.* Without *Him*, you cannot have *it.* And remember, you cannot receive the power of the Holy Spirit apart from the purity He imparts. Many would like to have the power but are not willing to be made pure. It would be dangerous for God to give His power to an impure person. This person would use it for selfish ends. God can only entrust His power to one who accepts His cleansing. Power is a by-product of purity.

Again, we must not seek power for the spectacular, the showy thing. This is the mistake that Simon Magus of Samaria made. The power of the Spirit is not for exhibition or self-glory. It is for service, for the glory of Christ. God can give His power only to those who are fully surrendered and dead to self. It's one thing to want the Holy Spirit so you can use *Him;* it's another thing to want Him so He can use *you.*

Finally, we must realize that we cannot receive the Pentecostal power unless we are willing to face the Pentecostal task. Pentecost for the disciples of Jesus began before they entered the upper room for prayer. It began when they accepted the responsibility of the Great Commission, when they ceased gazing upward into the skies on Mount Olivet and made their way back to Jerusalem. In doing so they faced their world of need, of danger, and of opportunity. Before that energizing experience in the upper room, the little band of disciples had already made plans for a forward thrust to carry Christ into the contemporary world. When they elected a disciple to take the place of Judas, they were looking in that direction. No doubt they were not ready for the task, but they had accepted the challenge.

God gives power only to men who need it and will put it to work. He doesn't waste power. He gives it to those who have tackled something so big, so overwhelming, that their own resources are quite insufficient. Such an acceptance of a challenge too big for human power is the opening of the door through which there comes the rushing of a mighty wind of the Spirit.

The parent acts in the same way toward a child who comes asking for money. What do you need it for? What do you plan to do with it? When we request a loan at the bank, the same question is asked.

When we ask God for power, these are the questions He puts to us: What are you going to do with it? Why do you need it? What responsibility have you faced? What challenge have you accepted? Are you utterly dependent upon this power?

Dr. Halford Luccock suggests that the reason for our lack of exhilaration and the conquering mood of Pentecost may lie in the fact that we are not planning to do anything in particular.

There are vast spiritual resources available to the Christian—resources for victorious living and effective witnessing. All he needs to do is to recognize that these resources do exist and they can be received personally by prayer, surrender, and faith.

In the days before rural electrification, a certain farmer went to the city and bought a book on electricity. He read it carefully and then decided to carry on a few simple experiments. First of all he set up a two-cell battery, attached some wires to it, and made an electric doorbell. He was delighted when he pushed the button and the bell rang. His first experiment was a success. Then he carried on some other minor experiments, and they too were successful. Finally he decided to electrify the whole house. So he put in all the equipment—the wiring, fixtures, and switches—and when the work was complete, with great anticipation he went to turn on the switch. But there were no lights. Disappointed, he sent to the city for the expert electrician. The man went over the equipment thoroughly, but could find no fault with the materials and the installation. Finally he turned to the farmer and said, "Sir, from where are you getting your power?"

The farmer then directed him to the two-cell battery with which he had first started his experiments. The electrician laughed and said, "That's enough power for a doorbell, but not for lights and appliances. However, let me tell you what to do. The main power line from the city runs in front of your farm not too far away. So if you apply to the electric company, they will connect you up with the main power line, and then you will have all the power you need."

Some of us are running our Christian lives on a two-cell battery; just enough power to make a little noise, but not enough for lights! God is saying to us, "Connect up with the main powerhouse and then you will have all the power needed for victory and service."

6

Rivers of Living Water

*The water that I shall give him will become in him a
spring of water welling up to eternal life. . . . Out of
his heart shall flow rivers of living water* (John 4:14;
7:38, RSV).

In these verses the Spirit-filled life is illustrated by
two figures. Jesus said to the woman at the well
of Sychar, "The water that I give is like a spring of
water." Then on the great day of the feast He stood
before the crowd and called out, "He who believes in
me . . . out of his heart shall flow rivers of living
water." Note: *in him a spring . . . out of him rivers.*

In us, the Holy Spirit is like a spring, an artesian
well, that is constantly fresh and never runs dry.

In the Old Testament we have the story of Hagar,
bondwoman of Abraham, who went out into the wil-
derness with her child, taking along a bottle of water.
In a short while the water was spent, and the mother,
greatly distressed, left her son in the bushes to die.
Then the record tells us that God opened the eyes of
Hagar, and she saw a well of water. She filled the bottle with water and gave the lad to drink (Gen.
21:9-21).

In the New Testament we have the story of the woman at the well of Sychar. She came with her waterpot, intending to draw water for her household needs. But she met the Master, and instead she found the water of life that He alone can give. So she left her waterpot behind and went home with the well inside of her (John 4:1-30).

God doesn't want us to be bottle Christians or waterpot Christians, but artesian-well Christians! This is what is meant by being filled with the Spirit.

Out of us, the Holy Spirit flows like a *river*—not a tricklet or a babbling brook, but a flowing river! In the Old Testament the psalmist says, "I will take the cup of salvation, and call upon the name of the Lord" (Ps. 116:13). But a cup is small and cannot hold very much. But the prophet Isaiah writes, "Therefore with joy shall ye draw out of the wells of salvation" (Isa. 12:3). A well is a great improvement over a little cup, but still there is the possibility of a well going dry. So when we come to the New Testament, Jesus tells us that the water which He gives will be in us "a spring of water welling up to eternal life" (John 4:14, RSV). A spring is fed by hidden sources and will never run dry. Then Jesus comes to the climax when He tells us that he that believes on Him, "out of his heart shall flow rivers of living water" (John 7:38, RSV). So the progression is from a cup to a well, from a well to a spring, and finally from a spring to a river. Here we see the vastness, the abundance of God's gift.

Then note, not just a river, but *rivers*. What divine prodigality! It is the Mississippi and Nile and Amazon all rolled into one. *Flowing* out of you—witness the freshness, the freedom, and the spontaneity of this flow. There is no pump work involved. Thus Christ promises to bestow a gift upon the one who receives Him as Saviour and Lord which will bring perfect satisfaction and sufficiency. Then through him will overflow rich blessing into the lives of others.

These two figures of the spring and rivers emphasize the extent of the incoming and outflowing of the Holy Spirit in our lives. The incoming of the Spirit is without measure. The Apostle John, in his Gospel, tells us that God gave to His Son His Spirit without measure (John 3:34). And we dare to believe that He desires to give the Spirit to every child of His without limitation. This is inferred from His promise given through the prophet Joel—"I will pour out my spirit upon all flesh" (Joel 2:28). The pouring suggests completeness.

This is what is meant by "the fulness of the Holy Spirit." We are to possess life, but more than that, the *abundant life*. We are to have joy, yea, the *fulness of joy*. We are to receive peace, even the *peace that passeth all understanding* (and misunderstanding too). We are to produce spiritual fruit, more than that, an *abundance of fruit*. This measures the difference between muddling through life and living life with abounding energy, abounding peace, and abounding power.

Likewise, the outflowing of the Holy Spirit is without measure—rivers shall flow. Life is *no longer a reservoir* with limited resources, so that if we draw on them we have only so much left, and therefore we must ration or conserve them. Life now becomes a channel attached to infinite resources, so there is no danger of exhausting the supply. We do not have to dole out our resources; for the more we give, the more we have. We are now living the inexhaustible life.

Within us the Holy Spirit abides like a spring. Out of us He flows like rivers.

Thus far we have been emphasizing the *infilling* of the Holy Spirit, but just as significant is the *outflowing* of the Spirit. May we suggest two reasons why it is necessary for the Holy Spirit to flow out of our lives.

1. TO KEEP US FRESH

A vessel may be filled with water, but if left standing, it becomes stagnant. In the same way, a person may be filled with the Holy Spirit, but unless there is continuous flow, he will soon become stale in the Christian life.

The story is told of a dear old brother who came regularly to the midweek prayer-and-praise service of his church and gave almost the same testimony week after week and month after month. The testimony went something like this: "Twenty-five years ago the Lord filled my cup up to the brim and it has been full ever since."

Every time the man stood to his feet, the people knew exactly what he was going to say. Apart from the periodic addition of a year, his witness hardly ever varied two or three words. Now it happened that a certain lady and her little girl were regular attenders at the prayer meeting and they heard this brother give the same old testimony over and over again. One Wednesday when he began the familiar words, "twenty-five years ago the Lord filled my cup and it's been full ever since," the little girl leaned over and whispered in her mother's ear, "Mother, I bet that man's cup is full of wiggle-tails!"

How true! There must be inflow and outflow to keep the supply fresh.

There is rhythm in the life of the Spirit—intake and outflow. If there is more intake than outflow, then the intake is blocked and ceases. If there is more outflow than intake, then the outflow stops, exhausted.

Several years ago, just after I had completed high school in India, our family was returning to the United States on our regular furlough. During the trip we had the privilege of visiting the little country of Palestine where our Lord had lived and labored. One day we went to see the famous Sea of Galilee. It is a beautiful lake with blue waters, surrounded by low hills. Many hamlets dotted the shoreline, and there were scores of fishermen plying up and down in their boats and catching an abundance of fish. The next day we went to the Dead Sea and spent an afternoon there. It is called the Dead Sea because it is so full of salt no fish or vegetable life can survive in it. The waters are so buoyant with salt that one can actually sit up in the water, hold an umbrella, and read a book.

The interesting fact about these two bodies of water

is that they are fed by the same streams that flow from snowcapped Mount Hermon. But why is it that the one is full of life and the other is called the Dead Sea? The secret is this. Several streams flow into the Sea of Galilee from the north, and at its southern end it empties its waters into the Jordan River. In other words, the Sea of Galilee takes in much water and gives out much water. Therefore it has life.

But as for the Dead Sea, much water flows into it but not a single little stream flows out. It takes in much water, but gives out nothing. The result? It is dead.

Unless we have both intake and outflow in our spiritual lives, the life that has been generated within us by the Holy Spirit will soon weaken and die. It takes the rhythm of both to keep us alive and fresh.

The Spirit-filled life is not static, fixed, or stationary. It is energetic, dynamic, progressive.

The infilling of the Holy Spirit is a definite *crisis*. But it is more than that. It is a *process* and a *state* as well. Note the three words or phrases that are used in the New Testament to describe the Spirit-filled life. It is recorded that on the Day of Pentecost the disciples were all "filled with" the Holy Spirit (Acts 2:4). From then on they are described as men "full of" the Holy Spirit (see Acts 6:5; 11:24). Then in Ephesians, Paul prays that the Christians may be "filled with all the fulness of God" (3:19). "Filled"—"full"—"filled with all the fulness"—these are the descriptive words. The first denotes a crisis; the second, a state or condition; and the third, a process.

First there is the *crisis*. There should be a definite time when we make a full surrender of ourselves, accept the gift of God by faith, and are *filled* with the Spirit for the first time in our lives. The disciples were with Christ for three years, but they were not filled with the Holy Spirit until the Day of Pentecost.

Then comes a *state* or *condition*. As long as we keep surrendered, obedient, and faithful, we can be men and women full of the Holy Spirit. For He comes, not as a transient Guest, but as a permanent Resident, to abide forever, as long as we provide the dwelling place.

The state is maintained by a *process*. There must be repeated infillings, so that we may be habitually full, taking in more and more of the fulness of God. To be spiritual one must be filled and kept filled. Thus we read of the apostles that after Pentecost they were filled on several occasions (see Acts 4:31, for example). Furthermore there is a certain enlargement that takes place in the spiritual life, so that we are able to contain more and more of the Spirit of Christ. Herein lies the growth aspect of the Christian life.

A study of the verb tenses used in the Greek language of the New Testament also brings out the truth of the three aspects of the Spirit-filled life. The *aorist* tense denotes a sudden, definite act of the past, something done and finished with. In Acts 2:4—"And they were all filled with the Holy Ghost"—the aorist tense is used, signifying *a definite historic crisis* of spiritual experience.

Then there is the *imperfect* tense, denoting just what it implies, an unfinished act. In Acts 13:52, "And the disciples were filled [literally, *were being filled*] with joy, and with the Holy Ghost"; and in Eph. 5:18, "Be filled [literally, *be being filled*] with the Spirit" —the imperfect tense is used, signifying a process, something that is still going on.

The *present* tense also denotes what it implies— action at the present moment. In Acts 7:55, it is recorded of Stephen: "Being full of the Holy Ghost, [he] looked up steadfastly into heaven." This is the present tense, denoting a current condition of fulness.

So there must be this continuous intake and outgo to keep us fresh and radiant in our daily lives. If we constantly take in without giving out, we become stagnant and then lifeless. This is the danger of the inactive church member. If we constantly give out without taking in, then we become dry and lifeless too. This is the great danger of the overly busy pastor or Christian worker.

Thus the correct illustration of the Spirit-filled life

is not one of a glass filled with water up to the brim and then left standing. Rather it is that of a glass with the bottom knocked out, then laid on its side on the bed of a stream, so that the water is constantly flowing in, the glass is always full, and the water is continuously flowing out.

2. To Make Us Fruitful

The infilling is not an end in itself. The Spirit flows *in* only so that He may flow *out*. As Dr. E. Stanley Jones says, "The Holy Spirit is like electricity. He never goes in where He can't come out."

The infilling of the Holy Spirit is for the supplying of *my own needs;* the outflowing is to help me supply *the needs of others.* The infilling is for *Christian character;* the outflowing is for *Christian conquest.* The infilling goes to my *innermost heart;* the outflowing goes to the *outermost world.*

There is a beautiful little prayer chorus that we often sing, "Spirit of the living God, fall fresh on me." In the original version of the chorus the middle line ran thus—"Melt me, break me, mold me, fill me." Then someone with spiritual insight saw there was something lacking in the chorus, and so changed this middle line to read: "Melt me, mold me, fill me, *use* me." He was right. The filling is not an end in itself, but only a means to usefulness.

There is a quaint parable about the rivers of the world. All the rivers met in a great convocation to decide which was the greatest river of all. The Nile River of Africa boasted, "I am the longest river in all the world, flowing for almost four thousand miles. Therefore I am the greatest."

The Amazon River of South America claimed with pride, "I am the widest river and have the greatest waterway system in the world, dumping 4,300,000,000 gallons of water hourly into the Atlantic Ocean. Therefore I am the greatest."

The Danube River of Europe said, "There is more commerce and there are more ships plying up and down my waters than on any other river. Therefore I am the greatest."

The Ganges River of India, not to be outdone, boasted of itself, "I am the holiest river in all the world. Thousands of people from all over the country come and bathe in my sacred waters to be cleansed of their sins. Therefore I am the greatest."

Finally, a little unnamed stream said meekly: "I am not the longest or the widest; I am not the busiest or the holiest. But this one thing I do. Every year I overflow my banks and give my water freely to the surrounding territory. The land becomes fertile; the crops grow; there is a great harvest; the people are fed and satisfied. I simply overflow."

In the opinion of the convocation this little stream was judged the greatest river of all, because it had learned to overflow and give of itself.

God intends for us to overflow and give of ourselves in fruitful service. This is why He fills us with the Holy Spirit.

A little girl said, "My heart is small and can't hold much of the love and grace of God. But it can overflow an awful lot!"

Let us be sure when we overflow that it is not *we* who are overflowing, but the *Spirit* who is overflowing through us. Nothing is so tragic as half-filled Christians trying to overflow. All that comes out is self, and that becomes very obnoxious. But when we are truly dead to self and completely filled with the Spirit, then the Spirit Himself flows out of our lives, and this makes us attractive and winsome. We become effective and fruitful in our Christian lives.

What is the fruit of the Spirit that is in evidence in the Spirit-filled life? The Apostle Paul very clearly describes this in his Epistle to the Galatians: "The fruit of the Spirit is love, joy, peace, patience, kindness, goodness, faithfulness, gentleness, self-control" (5:22-23, RSV). Notice, he says "fruit," not "fruits." The fruit of the Spirit is really one—LOVE. The rest of the list is merely a description of love in its various manifestations.

What is joy? It is love getting happy. What is peace? It is love in repose. What is patience? It is love in waiting. What is kindness? It is love in response. What is gentleness? It is love in behavior. What is faithfulness? It is love in trust. What is self-control? It is love in control.

Compare the virtues of love described in I Cor. 13:4-7 with the manifestations of love described in this passage in Galatians and it will be seen that every fruit of the Spirit is involved in this supernatural love. Indeed, either directly or by synonym, each of them is mentioned.

Love "suffereth long"—patience.

Love "is kind"—kindness.

Love "envieth not"—goodness.

Love "vaunteth not itself, is not puffed up"—gentleness.

Love "seeketh not her own, is not easily provoked" —self-control.

Love "rejoiceth in the truth"—joy.

Love "believeth all things, hopeth all things"—faithfulness.

Having love, we have all the fruit of the Spirit. Without love, we are nothing. "The love of God is shed abroad in our hearts by the Holy Ghost which is given unto us" (Rom. 5:5).

Thus the child of God is to be like a spring within and like rivers without. He is not to be a bottle Christian or a waterpot Christian, but an artesian-well Christian.

Too often we go to a retreat, or a revival, or a camp meeting, taking along our little waterpot, hoping to bring home a sufficient supply for the coming year, but expecting that the contents will grow less and less until driven by excessive thirst, we go back again next year to be revived again. God wants us to leave our waterpots behind and carry away the spring instead. The Spirit-filled life is one of satisfaction and sufficiency and surplus.

I once heard a humorous story about some Arabs

and an Englishman. I cannot vouch for its reliability, but I can testify to the spiritual lesson it conveys.

According to the story, an Englishman living in Cairo visited an Arab chief in Arabia. The guest was treated so royally and with such kindness that, on the eve of his departure, he invited the son of the desert to pay him a return visit to Cairo. He promised to put the Arab chief up in the finest hotel and to show him all the great sights of the city.

In the course of time the Arab chief and his retinue made the journey to Cairo. After allowing his guests a chance to rest, the Englishman went to the hotel to greet them. He knocked upon the door of the hotel room, but there was no response. He knocked several times, but still there was no answer. And yet he could hear voices within. So he quietly opened the door and slipped into the room. He found the chief and his group huddled together in the bathroom. They were turning the faucet on and off, splashing the water in their faces, and all the time talking excitedly like children.

The Englishman said, "Friends, it's time for us to be going. I want to show you all the great sights of Cairo —the pyramids, the Sphinx, the mosques, the museum, and so on."

The Arab chief answered, "Sir, we're not interested in all that. As you know, we come from Arabia, where water is as scarce as gold. But here is this little thing that you can turn any time of the day and night and get all the water you want. As far as we're concerned, this right here is the greatest sight in Cairo!"

On the last day the host came to say good-bye to the visitors. He knocked on the door of the hotel room, but again there was no response. So he quietly slipped into the room, and sure enough, he found the Arabs gathered in the bathroom again. There was a lot of commotion going on. One man had a pickaxe and was digging into the wall. Another was using a wrench on the pipe. Disturbed, the Britisher said, "What are you doing? You're destroying the hotel property. The manager will be most indignant. Please, please stop what you are doing."

The Arab chief calmly replied, "Friend, please don't be angry with us. We are returning to Arabia and you know how scarce water is in our country. We want to take this thing along with us, so we'll have all the water we want."

We laugh at the story, but many of us act the same way in our spiritual lives. Instead of connecting up with the reservoir, we just take the tap or a piece of the pipe along with us. In other words, instead of receiving the Holy Spirit in His fulness into our lives, we are satisfied with taking a little blessing, or a temporary emotional experience, or the overflow of someone else's supply. No wonder we soon run dry in our spiritual lives! God wants us to be channels attached to infinite resources, so that we may have an abundant supply for ourselves, and more than that, may have a surplus to share with others. We will not only be filled, but we will also overflow.

What are the conditions for this abundant spiritual life? Jesus, on the great day of the feast, stated them very clearly when He made His loving invitation to the people. He said, "If any man thirst, let him come unto me, and drink" (John 7:37).

Thirst is the first condition. The fulness of the Holy Spirit is offered to those who are spiritually thirsty. "Blessed are they which . . . thirst after righteousness: for they shall be filled." Thirst means consciousness of need and a genuine, heartfelt desire for that need to be met. Your fountain pen failed you yesterday; it would only scratch. What was wrong with it? It was dry. But it was not thirsty. It knew nothing of its need. Your car stopped dead the other day. Not a word of complaint had escaped concerning its growing need or the warning would have been taken. The tank was dry. Yet again, no thirst. There are many Christians who are dry also and, worse, are unconscious of their dryness. They must become thirsty—conscious of their need and desirous that it be met.

Drinking is the second condition. "Let the thirsty

come and drink," says the Master, who is the Giver of the water of life. What is drinking? It is simply receiving by faith. All the gifts of God are received by the hand of faith. It is by faith that we receive the gift of forgiveness and eternal life. It is also by faith that we receive the gift of the Spirit and power from on high.

Some years ago I was preaching at our annual jungle camp meeting in South India. This camp was started by my father and Rev. M. D. Ross back in 1923. Every year about six to seven thousand village Christians and "enquirers" assemble along the banks of a small stream, pitch their tents in the shade of the woods, set up their cooking facilities out under the trees, and attend the evangelistic services three times a day. For them it is the great spiritual feast of the year.

From its very inauguration the main teaching emphasis of this jungle camp meeting has been the fulness of the Holy Spirit. The key verse has been, "Tarry ye . . . until ye be endued with power from on high." The objective of the camp has been to produce a Spirit-filled ministry and laity and to equip the Indian Christians for effective witnessing and the evangelization of their own land. Down through the years the camp meeting has been the spearhead of a spontaneous people-movement that has brought close to one hundred sixty thousand people into the Kingdom and into the Church.

One morning after I had delivered the message, a sincere Christian came up to me and said, "You have talked about the fulness of the Holy Spirit. This is what I need. Will you please come out into the woods and pray with me?" (It has been our custom at the camp meeting, not to call people forward to an altar, but to urge them to go out among the trees and pray.) So I took my prayer rug and Bible and started off with him into the woods.

After he had gone a short way, the villager said to me. "Here is a lovely tree. Let's stop here and pray."

I said to him, "No, let's go on a little farther."

Still farther on, he said, "Sir, here is a beautiful mango tree with an abundance of shade. This would be a good place to pray."

Again I answered, "No, let's go on a little farther."

This went on for a while, the villager suggesting we stop and pray, and I insisting that we press on a little farther.

Suddenly the villager stopped, grabbed me by the hand, and said with all eagerness, "Sir, I don't know how far you are going, but I'm not going a step farther. I'm going to pray right here!"

I smiled, put my hand on his shoulder, and said, "Brother, be patient with me. I have just been testing you to see if you are really thirsty for the water of life, for only those who thirst shall be filled. I am now convinced that you are really thirsty. We need not go a step farther. This will be the place of your infilling."

We knelt in the shade of a tree, and lifted our voices together in prayer. This thirsty Christian came to Jesus and drank that morning until he was filled and satisfied, yea, until he began to overflow with joy and praise. And he drank, I am confident, until he was enabled to overflow into the lives of his family and community.

Is such a life yours? Do you sincerely desire this infilling? "If any man thirst"—that is the simple condition. "Let him come . . . and drink"—that is the loving invitation. Drink until you are satisfied, until you are full, yea, until you overflow. The fulness of the Holy Spirit is for everyone who thirsts and drinks of the water of life.

In you the Spirit will be as a spring. Out of you He shall flow as rivers.

7

Fanning the Flame

Quench not the Spirit (I Thess. 5:19).

Never damp the fire of the Spirit (Phillips).

In his First Epistle to the Thessalonians, the Apostle Paul ends the letter with a series of terse, pungent exhortations and warnings. It is as if he were handing us a bunch of telegrams. Note, for example, "Rejoice always, pray constantly, give thanks for all circumstances . . . test everything; hold fast what is good, abstain from every form of evil" (RSV).

In the middle of these pointed statements is this grave warning: "Quench not the Spirit." It is a four-word telegram to every child of God.

The key word is the initial word, "quench." A very interesting word it is in the original language. It is what we call a picture word. It suggests one in the act or process of putting out a flame, so that a simple rendering of this verse could be: "Don't put out the fire of the Holy Spirit." That suggests something that is by no means unfamiliar to students of the Word. Over and over again in the Holy Scriptures this natural phenomenon, so full of mystery, that we call fire is used as a symbol of the Divine Presence and of God's redemptive word in the human heart.

In the Old Testament we find instance after instance in which this symbol is used: fire at the burning bush when Moses met the great I AM; fire in the holy of holies in the Tabernacle; fire coming in the form of a live coal to touch the lips of the young prophet, Isaiah, and equip him for his future ministry.

We find that the same symbolism persists in the New Testament, with this one difference: that whereas in the Old Testament fire is a general symbol of God's nature and energy, in the New Testament fire is particularly a symbol of the Third Person of the Trinity, the Holy Spirit. At the very threshold of the Gospels we are presented with this fact. John the Baptist, speaking to his converts on the banks of the Jordan River, said: "I indeed baptize you with water unto repentance but he that cometh after me is mightier than I, whose shoes I am not worthy to bear: he shall baptize you with the Holy Ghost, and with fire" (Matt. 3:11). That was both prophecy and promise. On the Day of Pentecost it was fulfilled in the lives of the disciples. And the experience was duplicated in the lives of others as recorded by the historian Luke.

Scripture after Scripture incorporates this symbol which is suggested in the passage: "Don't put out the fire of the Holy Spirit." Fire illuminates; so does the Holy Spirit. Fire energizes; so does the Holy Spirit. Fire refines; so does the Holy Spirit. Fire fuses, welds, unites; so does the Holy Spirit. These are points that quickly come to mind as we press this interesting parallelism between fire and the Holy Spirit.

Now in the realm of our relationship to the Holy Spirit, Paul is simply recognizing that the Spirit of God is a living presence. He speaks of Him as fire, not merely to symbolize His ministry of cleansing and empowering, but mainly His living, energizing presence. He is emphasizing that this is a person-to-person relationship. And it is just here that the danger arises. In the realm of moral relationships and spiritual experiences, the realm in which the Spirit of God deals with us and we respond to Him, it is alarmingly possible for us to hinder and hurt. Here it is that you can do what you cannot do in other areas of life. For example, you can go out at high noon on a cloudless day and shake your fist in defiance of the sun and its shining rays, and nothing comes of it. God is sovereign in that phase of nature, and you can do nothing about it. But when God shines in your direction, into your heart and mind, by the light of the Holy Spirit, you can, if you choose, prevent that light from reaching you and doing you any good. In other words, the human in this realm can frustrate the divine; the finite can hinder the infinite.

It is this very danger that is uppermost in the mind of Paul when he gives us this warning. "Therefore," he says, "be careful. Have care how you treat the Holy Spirit and His gracious ministries. *Quench not the Spirit.*"

How is it possible for us to quench the Spirit? I believe there are three important passages in the New Testament in each of which is revealed some particular phase of the active ministry of the Holy Spirit, and in connection with which we may see how it is possible for us to put out the Spirit's fire.

In Acts 5:32 we read these words: "And we are his witnesses of these things; and so is also the Holy Ghost, whom God hath given to them that obey him."

The significant word here is "witnesses." The ministry of the Holy Spirit is linked up with witnessing. Paul would say, "Don't put out the Spirit's testimony flame."

Recall the circumstances under which these words were spoken. Peter was the spokesman representing John and other Spirit-filled ones who had been challenged by the authorities. These apostles had been bearing such a powerful witness to Jesus Christ that the whole city was being stirred by it. They had been ordered to cease this "Jesus propaganda" and had been threatened with punishment if they failed to obey. Taking absolutely no notice of these threatenings, they had gone right on, bearing their testimony before the people. Now they are before the magistrates again, and this is the charge: "Did not we straitly command you that ye should not teach in this name? and, behold, ye have filled Jerusalem with your doctrine, and intend to bring this man's blood upon us" (Acts 5:28). Blessed compliment! In other words, "You have not silenced your testimony."

To that Peter makes brave answer, "We ought to obey God rather than men."

We see in that word "ought" a flame of fire. It should stir our hearts as it stirred the hearts of those disciples that day. Peter is not speaking for himself merely, but for all those who are witnesses. "Sir, do you ask us to silence our witness for Jesus? Never! Christ has done so much for us. He has been made so real to us. He has so captured our personalities. He has so won our allegiance that when you say we must not speak in His name, you are putting your finger on the dearest thing in our lives. We can't stop. It is fire in our bones."

Do you say, "I never felt anything like that"? Don't say that unless you mean to say that you have never had a real experience of Jesus Christ. If Christ really gets hold of you, He will kindle this fire of witnessing in your heart, especially if you are filled with the Holy Spirit and know the deeper meaning of Christ's redeeming grace and the power of His divine Paraclete working in you.

When a person is born of the Spirit and becomes a child of God, he partakes of the nature and spirit of the Heavenly Father. The Father is concerned over lost children; His heart goes out in compassion to them; He passionately desires their salvation; He is actively engaged in the work of seeking and saving the lost. This concern and compassion are shed abroad in the heart of the believer by the Holy Spirit, who is given unto him. The believer now wants to share Christ with everyone—with his family members, his neighbors, and his fellow laborers. He takes great joy in telling others what Christ has done for him and what He can do for all who put their trust in Him. In other words, the flame of testimony is kindled upon the altar of his heart.

The baptism with the Holy Spirit adds fuel to this flame. The Spirit delivers the believer from cowardice and the fear of man. He increases the desire to share Christ with others. He empowers with new strength and unction for the task. Jesus said to His disciples, "You shall receive power when the Holy Spirit has come upon you; and you shall be my witness" (Acts 1:8, RSV). Witnessing thus becomes the spontaneous outflow of the Spirit's fulness.

But it is possible for us to quench the testimony flame in our hearts. We can quench the flame by *preoccupation*. It is possible for a minister to become so involved in the machinery of the church—running the commissions and committees, conducting the services, raising the budget, marrying and burying, making out the reports—that he has no time left for the primary spiritual ministries of the pastorate, especially for witnessing and personal work. In time he dulls the keen edge of his evangelistic drive.

A layman may become so preoccupied with his own personal interests, with his efforts to make an adequate living and supply himself with the comforts of modern life, that he too finds he has no time to converse with his friends and neighbors about spiritual matters. Soon he begins to rationalize and say within himself, Well, after all, this is the business of the pastor. That's what he gets paid for. So why should I worry? In a short while the flame of witnessing has become a dying ember.

A young businessman who attended one of our summer "Ashrams" (retreats) got up and said this in the "Hour of the Open Heart": "Friends, I want to confess that I have been cheating my comrades down at the office." Most of us thought he was talking about money at first, but he went on to explain, "I have failed to tell them about Christ and what He has done for me."

We can quench the Spirit's testimony flame by over-tactfulness. We don't want to offend anyone; we don't want to seem overbearing; we don't want to be guilty of pressuring anyone; or we're so afraid we'll do or say the wrong thing. And so we employ so much *tact* that we lose *contact*. We end up doing nothing. We throw water on the Spirit's flame.

A few years ago when my wife and I were missionaries in India, stationed in the city of Balgaum, in the state of Mysore, one evening we made a friendly call on the collector and his family. The collector is the chief executive of the entire political district, and so is a man of authority and prestige. He is always a person of education and culture. This particular collector was a Hindu by religion, and quite orthodox in belief and practice. When my wife and I arrived at their beautiful home, the collector greeted us very graciously and said, "We're so happy you have come. You are the very first visitors since the birth of our new child. You must come and see the mother and baby."

He took us up to the bedroom, and there we saw the happy mother and the beautiful child lying in her arms. It was a boy, perfectly formed and bright-eyed. How proudly the parents showed him off!

As I stood by the bedside talking to the father and mother, I had an inward impression that I should offer prayer for the new baby and ask God's blessings upon him and his parents. But then I thought to myself, But they are Hindus. Maybe they won't appreciate a Christian minister praying for them. The father is the collector, the chief official of the district. Maybe he'll be offended. And so, sad to say, I listened to my own thoughts rather than the voice of the Spirit. I failed to pray.

When we left the house and headed for home, my wife said to me, "Honey, as we stood there by the bedside of that mother and child, I had a strong impression that you should offer a prayer for them. We were the first visitors, and missionaries at that. Why didn't you pray? It was such a wonderful opportunity for a witness."

My wife merely put words to what the Spirit was saying quietly within me. When we reached home, I went alone to my office, shut the door, and fell on my knees. "Lord, forgive me," I prayed. "I failed You in the moment of opportunity to witness before a high official. Help me never to miss another chance to witness for You."

John Fletcher, speaking particularly about the obligation of sharing the fulness of Christ with others, has left us the unhappy acknowledgement—a great humiliation it was—that at five different times he lost the witness to his experience of perfect love simply because he was afraid to testify to it. It will convict anyone to read the entire testimony he bears, how he allowed the attitudes of certain people and the subtle arguments of Satan to defeat him, and how the fire went out.

If Christ has redeemed us, if He lives and reigns in our hearts, let us tell it wherever we go. William James, the psychologist, taught that no worthy impression should ever go without its appropriate expression. Someone else has aptly reminded us that "impression minus expression equals depression."

What does this mean? It means you must not put out the flame of witnessing. If you do not give the vision splendid voice, then the vision will fade. The unacknowledged blessing withers in the heart. The shut-in flame goes out for want of a draft. Don't quench the Spirit's testimony.

THE PRAYER FLAME

In his Epistle to the Romans, Paul writes: "Likewise the Spirit helps us in our weakness; for we do not know how to pray as we ought, but the Spirit himself intercedes for us with sighs too deep for words" (8:26, RSV).

Here the ministry of the Holy Spirit is linked up with the prayer life of the believer. When a person is born of the Spirit, along with the flame of testimony the flame of prayer is also lit. The believer desires to tell others of Christ. He also desires to commune with the Father daily.

The point that Paul is making in this particular verse is that you cannot have real prayer apart from the Holy Spirit. Paul says, left to ourselves, relying upon ourselves and our own resources, we know neither the how nor the what of real prayer, but God knows our human weakness and therefore has given unto us the Holy Spirit to help us.

The Spirit gives us both the *impulse* and the *insight* for prayer. So far as the impulse is concerned, it may be either ordinary or extraordinary: ordinary, in that gentle, persuasive push of the mind toward communion with God; extraordinary in those special burdens of prayer, the sense of soul travail, of great and intense exercising of the spirit in prayer. But whether it be the common or uncommon impression, heed it. This is the work of the Spirit.

The Spirit also supplies the prayer *insight*. He reveals to you the line along which your prayer is to proceed in harmony with the purposes of God. No prayer that is real is out of harmony with the will of God. Prayer guidance is essential. Guidance in a special form comes through that direct influence of the Spirit upon our hearts, that play upon the minds of men. It is the inner voice of the Holy Spirit.

Like the testimony flame, the prayer flame also may be dampened by preoccupation. There are so many duties to perform, we are so busy, that we just seem to have no time for prayer. And so we allow the daily routine, the pressures of modern life, to crowd out the quiet time. Soon the prayer flame is snuffed out.

I shall never forget the case of a missionary to India who almost completely extinguished the prayer flame in his life and was on the verge of leaving the ministry. I was a lad of fifteen, studying in the American high school at Kodaikanal, in the beautiful hills of south India. It was in the month of May, when missionaries of all denominations, from all across the southern half of the peninsula, came to the hills for their summer vacation. That year a trio of young evangelists from the United States were holding special revival services for the missionaries and students. It was a blessed time for spiritual renewal.

One day after the morning service the speaker gave an invitation to those with a spiritual need to come into the inquiry room for counsel and prayer. Conscious of my own need, I went in along with several others. Most of the group were praying rather quietly, but suddenly one of the brethren seemed to forget himself and began to pray rather loudly. One could sense the deep burden and strong emotion that laid hold of him. I shall never forget his prayer. It was the strangest prayer I have ever heard. He started off with these words: *"Lord, I've been such a jackass!"* And then he went on to confess how for the past seven years he had not spent time with the Lord in the place of prayer. Oh, yes, he had prayed in public when he was conducting the regular worship service, or when he was called upon to lead in prayer, but he had not taken time all those years to keep up his own private devotional life. As a result, he was defeated in his inner life and discouraged about the work. He had already written to the mission board back home, sending in his resignation.

That day the missionary made a new surrender of himself to God and a new determination not to allow anything in the future to keep him from his quiet time with God. Once again the Spirit lighted the flame of prayer in his heart. He withdrew his resignation, stayed on at his post of duty, and entered into a more effective ministry for the Master. I still recall the testimony of victory which he gave in one of the midweek prayer services the following summer. He testified that it had been the best year of his life. The prayer flame was now ablaze.

Suppose when there comes an impulse from the Spirit to pray, I am negligent, I am preoccupied. The mischief of that sort of thing is that it tends to repeat itself. After a while, what then? I quench the Spirit. I damp the fire.

Now this does not mean that the first time a person is a bit negligent in regard to his prayer life, the Holy

Spirit is going to walk off and leave him. He is not that kind of Person. He is not some kind of capricious policeman peeping around the corner all the time waiting for some provocation to desert us. He is a long-suffering Spirit, extremely tender in all His dealings with us. Immediately there is any sign of letting down, He will gently reprove and admonish us. But, to repeat, the mischief of this sort of carelessness is that it tends to repeat itself and, before long if we are not careful, the fire has gone out. When our prayer life has been neglected, the moral defenses of our souls are down, and all manner of temptations may tramp in upon us. Soon defeat stalks into the sanctuary of our lives, leaving upon the neglected altar the ashes of a once glowing prayerfulness.

Paul would admonish us: "Don't put out the Spirit's prayer flame."

THE LOVE FLAME

In his Epistle to the Ephesians, the fourth chapter, and the last verses, the Apostle Paul admonishes his readers thus: "Grieve not the Holy Spirit of God, whereby ye are sealed unto the day of redemption. Let all bitterness, and wrath, and anger, and clamour, and evil speaking, be put away from you, with all malice: and be ye kind one to another, tenderhearted, forgiving one another, even as God for Christ's sake hath forgiven you."

In other words, Paul is saying, "Do not put out the Spirit's love flame. Be careful how you treat the Spirit of God in His ministry of love."

As we have seen previously, the fruit (not fruits) of the Spirit is love. The other virtues are merely phases of love. Love is the inclusive and indispensable Christian grace. It is the master grace, the key to all of life. Therefore if you fail at the point of love, you have failed where failure is tragic. It makes no difference what else you have to your credit. If the love flame goes out, your inner life becomes a crater, just an old shell.

Paul makes it clear that *bitterness* is fatal to this love fire glowing in your heart. For instance, suppose one of your close friends does something you think he should not have done, and instead of committing it to God as a Spirit-filled Christian should, you chafe under it. You brood over it. The more you dwell on it, the more uncomfortable you become. The first thing you know, censoriousness has come in through a crack in the door of your heart; and once it creeps in, it plays a steady stream of cold water on the flame of your love. Then what?

When you are rankling on the inside with resentment, it does not take much provocation for that feeling to seek expression in some hasty, caustic word or attitude. What next? Evil speaking. Oh, what unkindness, what unfairness, what cruelty come from tongues loosed from the sweet restraints of love! Suddenly you awaken to the fact that love as a flame has died out, been extinguished. Kindness and tenderness are gone. Forbearance and charity are gone. What was once a kindling flame of glowing beauty has become a smoldering ember.

Several years ago the missionaries of a certain denomination in Korea were gathered together for their annual business session. In that conference a certain problem was being debated, and two missionaries differed as to the solution. Each one argued for his side of the question. At first the discussion was friendly and everything went on in a true Christian spirit. The two men simply did not see eye to eye, and each was seeking to prove his point. But it went on until one of them got out of the Spirit. In an unguarded moment he spoke harsh words, words of bitterness and accusation against his brother. Immediately the other man responded in the same spirit. It put a cloud upon the whole conference. The two men returned to their respective stations with a residue of bitterness lodged in their hearts.

Sad though the situation was, the aftermath was glorious. It began when one of the men was in prayer one day, beseeching the Lord about a series of special meetings they were planning at the mission station. He had not been praying very long until the Spirit of God spoke to him reprovingly. "There is no use for you to pray for a revival here until you first be reconciled to your brother."

The rebuke was so strong that the next morning, bright and early, he was on a slow-going train to the other mission station, a hundred miles away. When he arrived there he asked to see the other brother and they went alone into a room. The visitor said, "I have not come to finish the debate. I have not come to place blame, but to take blame. God has reproved me for the attitude I took toward you and the words I spoke. I want you to forgive me. I have grieved the Spirit."

You can guess what happened. The other man broke down and said, "I was as much to blame as you were, and I want to ask you to forgive me."

They embraced and then got on their knees and asked God's forgiveness, invoking His blessing and power upon their lives. The next day they separated as brethren, with the love fire glowing in their hearts. When the news got out that the missionary had made the 100-mile journey to confess his bitterness and had been reconciled to his brother missionary, it shook the whole station. Other people began to make confessions and to set things right before God and between themselves. A genuine revival came to that station, and the glorious thing was that the revival fire leaped the gap and ignited the mission station of the other brother with a new flame. Many Christian workers were spiritually revived, and many non-Christians were won to Christ.

We must allow nothing to quench the flame of love upon the altars of our hearts, for love is the supreme virtue of the Christian life. On the other hand, as Paul exhorts the church in Thessalonica, we need to increase and abound more and more in this love which is shed abroad in our hearts by the Holy Spirit.

Several years ago Dr. E. Stanley Jones was engaged in an extended preaching mission all across the

United States. Every night he spoke in a different church. He soon found himself observing very carefully what the various pastors of these churches had hidden behind their pulpits. Behind one was a glass of water. Dr. Jones commented, "A drink before the message would probably keep the sermon from being dry."

Behind another pulpit he noticed a wastepaper basket. "Many of our sermons," he observed, "should probably go in [the basket] if they don't *go over* [with the congregation]."

In another pulpit the pastor kept a thermometer. Dr. Jones reflected, "You can't tell the spiritual temperature of a church with an ordinary thermometer."

In another place he noticed a couple of wads of chewing gum on the pulpit. He remarked, "This represents the moving of the jaw, but not necessarily the moving of the mind."

But to top it all off, in one church Dr. Jones noticed a small fire extinguisher placed inside the pulpit! He commented in all seriousness, "This is the tragedy of the Church today and of many a Christian. We have been using the fire extinguisher to put out the flame of the Holy Spirit. We need to quit dampening and begin fanning the flame."

The Apostle Paul admonishes us: "Don't put out the Spirit's testimony flame. Don't quench the prayer flame. Don't extinguish the love flame."

When government engineers were engaged in the Tennessee Valley Authority project, the construction of one of the large dams was being hindered by an old, weather-beaten shack that stood in the way. An old Tennessee mountaineer lived in that shack, and he had no mind to move. The engineers offered to pay compensation for the house far above its value. But still the occupant held his ground. He didn't want the money; he wanted his shack.

In curiosity the engineers asked him one day, "What makes you want to hold on to this old dilapidated shack? With the money we are offering you,

you could build a fine house and live comfortably the rest of your life."

Finally the old mountaineer told the secret. He took them into the house, and pointing to the fireplace, he said, "You see that fire? My grandfather started that fire and he never let it go out during his whole lifetime. My father kept that fire burning all his life too. And I intend to keep it going the rest of my life. That fire means too much to me to let go of this house."

The engineers never said a word, but they immediately set to work constructing a new house for the mountaineer on the other side of the hill. One day when the mountaineer was out, they slipped into his shack, scooped up some of the live coals from the fireplace, and with them kindled a new fire on the hearth of the new home. Then they brought the old man and showed him what they had done. They were able to convince him that this was the continuation of his own fire and that he could keep it going the rest of his life. Then only did he consent to move.

So we too must keep the fire of the Holy Spirit burning upon the altars of our hearts.

Keep the *testimony* flame burning. Keep the *prayer* flame ablaze. Keep the *love* flame glowing.

8

A Modern Pentecost

Thus far we have been making a detailed study of the significance of the Holy Spirit in the life of the believer. We have sought to discover who the Holy Spirit is, what His ministry is in the world, what it means to be filled with the Holy Spirit, and what the results of His indwelling presence are. We have pursued our study mainly through the teachings of the Scriptures and through the lives of the early Christians.

The questions which now arise are: Does what we have been saying so far have any relevance to the church in the twentieth century? Is Pentecost possible today on a scale comparable with that of the Early Church? Does the enduement with power from on high have any significance for widespread evangelism and for the growth of the Church?

In seeking to answer these questions, the argument of mere words will not suffice. The argument of history and experience is far more convincing. And so we present a descriptive account of modern Pentecost that took place in India in this very twentieth century.

When my father, Earl Arnett Seamands, sailed as a Methodist missionary to India on August 23, 1919, two outstanding spiritual experiences in his life were destined to determine the nature and pattern of his future missionary career.

The first was his experience at Camp Sychar, in Mount Vernon, Ohio, in the summer of 1912. Since his conversion and call took place in the atmosphere of an old-fashioned camp meeting, the camp meeting as an effective method of evangelism captured his heart and mind. He began to read avidly the history of the camp meeting movement in the United States. An eyewitness account of the famous Cane Ridge, Kentucky, camp meeting of 1801 had special and lasting influence upon his thinking. Dad began to ask himself the questions, Why can't God duplicate such an experience even today? And if He can do it in America why not in India?

The second experience took place in the winter of 1915 while Dad was still an engineering student in the University of Cincinnati. From messages preached at Camp Sychar and at his newly found church-home at Wesley Chapel in Cincinnati, Dad had heard of the possibility of a personal experience of Pentecost in the heart of the believer. A study of the Scriptures and a careful analysis of his own spiritual need convinced him of the necessity of the fulness of the Holy Spirit in his own life. As a result he began earnestly to seek this experience. After about a week of fasting and prayer, Dad was walking from the campus of the University toward the sidewalk on Clifton Avenue at about seven o'clock in the evening. It was the seventh day of January, 1915. There was snow on the ground; darkness had already settled down upon the city. A silent conversation was going on between the Lord and the young engineer. Dad said, "Lord, I know I'm fully surrendered to You. I want Your will more than anything else—more than my engineering career, my marriage, my ambitions. Lord, what lack I yet?"

The Lord answered with just one word—"Faith."

Dad prayed from his heart, "Lord, give me this faith."

And then it happened! The place around Dad seemed to be bathed in a divine light. He was overwhelmed with a feeling of indescribable peace and joy. The doubts were swept away; a quiet assurance filled his heart. Christ had baptized with the Holy Spirit and with fire! Dad went to the dormitory, put on an extra pair of pants and a heavy sweater, went out to the bandstand in the park, knelt down and prayed for a long time, thanking God for the gift of the fulness of the Holy Spirit.

Thus when the young missionary-engineer arrived at his destination in India on October 3, 1919, two great spiritual ambitions had control of his heart and mind: (1) to inaugurate the camp meeting movement in India and (2) to witness a repetition of Pentecost in the life of the Indian church. It was four years before he was to see these two ambitions fulfilled, but these were important years of orientation, adjustment, and language study.

Meanwhile the divine-human factors were all taking shape under the influence of the Holy Spirit. Dad had completed his language study and was now appointed superintendent of Bidar District, an interior, rural area. In the district adjoining, namely, Vikarabad District, another young missionary, Rev. M. D. Ross, was the superintendent. Ross and Seamands had made one another's acquaintances just two years previous and from the moment they met their hearts began to beat in unison.

Like Dad, Ross had been converted in a camp meeting in the United States (a camp in Kansas). Like Dad, he too had trusted in God for his personal Pentecost and believed strongly in the necessity of the Spirit-filled life. This resulted in a David-and-Jonathan-like spirit of friendship, and a Paul-and-Barnabas-like team of evangelism between these two young missionaries.

Then came November, 1923. Ross and Seamands agreed that they would attempt a miniature camp meeting at a site midway between the two districts. The dates: November 15 to 23. The location: a wooded area between Bidar and Tandur, where there was a large unused well, known as "Bondla Bhavi" (the traveler's well).

The strategy was for both missionaries carefully to choose and bring from their respective districts the top-level Indian workers, conference members, and local preachers of good experience, along with their wives. There was just one aim in the mind of the two missionaries—to "tarry until" the entire group was filled with the Holy Spirit. They believed that if the main leaders were revived and endued with power, the spiritual impact would be felt throughout the whole ministry and laity as well.

Thus it was that on the opening day of the camp about one hundred of the district preachers and their wives met together at Bondla Bhavi. A few laymen from nearby villages joined the group and brought the total number to approximately 150. Some stayed in tents; some built simple brush arbors; others improvised temporary shelters out of bamboo mats. Each family managed its own cooking on outdoor fireplaces. And so the first "jungle camp meeting" was under way.

At first the campers were confused. "What are we doing out here in the jungle?" they asked. "There are nothing but tigers and cobras here. What are these crazy missionaries up to anyway? Do they want us to die?"

"Yes," answered the two young missionaries, "We've come here to die. Not in the physical sense, however, but in the spiritual sense."

And soon the campers began to understand as they heard over and over the slogan of the camp meeting: "Die to sin; receive the Holy Spirit; live unto righteousness."

There were three services a day, with Ross and Seamands alternating as speakers. On the authority of God's Word, backed by personal testimony, the two missionaries expounded "the way of God more perfectly," emphasizing the Christian's obligation and privilege of being filled with the Spirit. No altar call was given, but after each message the people were urged to go out alone under the trees and pray specifically for the baptism with the Spirit. If the assurance of victory came to anyone, he was urged to return to the camp and share his experience in personal testimony with the rest of the group.

For the first three days nothing visible happened, but a deep sense of conviction and heart-hunger gripped the campers. Then on the afternoon of the third day the first victory took place. One of the Telegu-speaking preachers, A. S. Abraham by name, became so desperate in his search that he sought out Mr. Ross and asked him to come out under a tree and pray with him. Before they arose from their knees, the Spirit came in glorious fulness. That evening Abraham stood in the service and gave a clear-cut testimony to the baptism with the Holy Spirit in his life.

This testimony lit a spark of expectancy in the hearts of the others. The next afternoon the second victory took place. Rev. Jotappa Jacob, a conference member, went out to his prayer tree after lunch, determined that he would not return until he had received the Holy Spirit in His fulness. His eye fell upon the words in Luke 11:13—"How much more shall your heavenly Father give the Holy Spirit to them that ask him?" He closed the Book, bowed his head, and just asked God to give him the Holy Spirit. Suddenly his heart was strangely warmed, and Jacob jumped to his feet shouting, "He has come; the Holy Spirit has come!" He ran through the woods looking for someone to tell about what had happened. That evening in the service Jacob shared his testimony with the whole group, and was followed by two other Indian men whom he had led into the new experience during the afternoon hours.

Other victories quickly followed. Rev. N. S. Samson told the group of a vision he had had during the previous night. It seemed as if a fire had broken out in the camp. It started at the missionaries' tent and began to spread until it consumed the whole camp. He said he awoke and all seemed to be light about him. Whether this was really a vision or a dream or neither, it is a parable which pictures quite well what took place during the next few days. To Samson it was a transforming experience.

Perhaps the most significant victory, next to Rev. Jotappa Jacob's, was that of Rev. Krishnayya, an ordained elder in the Bidar District. He confided to the group, "I have studied about the Holy Spirit; I have preached about the Holy Spirit; but never did I realize as now that I have not yet received Him in His fulness. I must receive Him or I cannot live."

My father gave him a promise or two from the Word and urged him to go alone into the woods and pray. Before the service was over, Krishnayya returned. The light on his countenance was the testimony of what had taken place. And from then on, the spiritual fire began to sweep through the camp. Krishnayya and Jacob seemed to become the natural leaders of the movement, under the anointing of the Holy Spirit. The other campers began to come to them for guidance and prayer; little prayer groups sprang up all over the woods.

The two missionaries were momentarily pushed into the background of the picture. But this is exactly what they had prayed for and longed to see—the Holy Spirit taking possession of the Indian preachers, and the church going forward under their leadership. Now it was no longer the foreign missionary telling what had happened to him in some camp meeting in America; it was an Indian brother telling his own people what had happened to him on Indian soil. This was truly an Indian Pentecost taking place in the twentieth century.

By the end of the week in that historic month of November, 1923, almost every one of the 150 persons present could testify with assurance to the abiding presence of the Holy Spirit.

What took place at Bondla Bhavi was by no means superficial; it was genuine. It was no temporary outburst of emotion; it was a permanent transformation of life. The results were manifest in the lives of individuals and in the spirit of the entire conference. To this very day, more than forty years later, there are evidences of the permanent results of the first camp meeting throughout the work of the South India and Hyderabad conferences.

When the camp broke up on the twenty-third of November, the two missionaries, Ross and Seamands, and the district workers returned to their various places of duty to get ready for district conference. On his way home Dad began to develop a temperature, and the next day he was delirious with a high fever. The missionary doctor, Dr. Charles Pinckney, diagnosed it as a serious case of typhus. For twenty-three days Dad hung in the balance between life and death. During this period he lost thirty pounds. But he still held on in faith that God would raise him up to see further evidences of Pentecost.

Because of his illness, Dad had to turn over the conducting of the Bidar District Conference to two of his Indian colleagues, Rev. N. E. Samson and Rev. Jotappa Jacob. These two brethren, fresh in their new spiritual experience gained at the camp meeting, were more concerned about spiritual revival than they were about the passing of resolutions. They both shared their newfound experience with the members of the district conference and urged each one to "tarry until" he was endued with power from the Holy Spirit.

The result was repetition of what took place at the jungle camp meeting—a new outpouring of the Holy Spirit. Revival fires swept through the group and then spread out into the district.

Meanwhile in Vikarabad District nearby, where Rev. M. D. Ross was the superintendent, a similar movement was taking place. The members of the district conference experienced their personal Pentecost and then went back to their homes and churches to spread the good news.

All this time Dad was battling for his very life. Annual conference was to take place shortly and he desired so much to be able to attend the conference session and tell the news of the revival that was sweeping that section of the work. On his bed he prayed earnestly, "Lord, if You will enable me to get to annual conference, I will bear witness to Your grace."

The Lord said, "I'll raise you up, but when you get to conference you must ask everyone you contact the apostolic question, 'Have you received the Holy Spirit?' " It was not an easy assignment, but Dad accepted the challenge.

Meanwhile the news of the outpouring of the Holy Spirit at Bondla Bhavi camp and at the Bidar and Vikarabad district conferences had spread through the rest of the South India Conference area. So when the members of the Conference gathered together in early January, 1924, at Kolar Town, there was a strong spirit of expectancy that permeated the atmosphere.

From the very beginning of the sessions there was an unusual sense of the presence of the Holy Spirit in their midst. The delegates from Bidar and Vikarabad began to share their testimony with the other delegates. Each evening Dad and Mr. Ross conducted informal prayer-and-witness meetings in the Bible school building.

Remembering his promise made to the Lord, Dad went from person to person, both missionary and national, and asked the apostolic question, "Have you received the Holy Spirit?" It took a lot of courage to go up to the presiding bishop, Bishop Frank W. Warne, and put the question to him. But the good bishop smiled and said, "Yes, Brother Seamands, thank God I have received the Holy Spirit. Hallelujah!"

And then he told how some years ago in his homeland in Canada he had received the fulness of the Spirit.

The movement of the Spirit at the south India conference session followed a rather unusual pattern. Each night the Holy Spirit came upon a different language group. The first night the Telegu-speaking members received their Pentecost; the next night, the Kanarese-speaking delegates; the third night, the Tamil-speaking group.

Finally the movement broke through the conference

delegation and touched the local Methodist Girls' School. Informal services were held nightly in the school hall and many of the young girls came into a new experience with Christ. In this way the annual conference of 1924 proved to be a great revival conference that brought new spiritual life and power to the leadership of Methodism in south India.

The revival left its lasting impressions upon the missionaries and Indian ministers, so that down through the years South India Conference (now divided into Hyderabad and South India conferences) has always sought to maintain a high standard of Christian purity and ethics, and has always sought to keep evangelism at the very center of its life and work. Spiritual revival has been a keynote of its conference objectives.

Meanwhile back in Bidar District a new phase of the spiritual movement was developing. So far the outpouring of the Holy Spirit had been confined, for the most part, to the leadership of the conference—to missionary and ordained preacher. The supply preachers and the village laity had not been touched. The latter began to ask questions: What is the gift of the Holy Spirit? Is this gift only for the American missionary and for the Indian conference member? Is God a respecter of persons? Soon they were to receive God's own answer to their inquiry.

T. C. Veeraswamy was a local preacher who had been present at the Bandla Bhavi camp meeting and had received his personal Pentecost. Dad had left the District Training School in this man's hands while he was away at annual conference. Veeraswamy set the Training School ablaze with revival and then headed for the villages, where, under the inspiration of the Spirit, he developed a technique all of his own.

He selected a strategically located village and urged the local Christians to contribute enough rice and rations to feed a large group of people for one day. Then the Christians from the neighboring villages were invited to join the local group in a one-day revival.

The villagers were requested to be present by early

afternoon and were assembled in a shady grove of trees some distance from the village. Veeraswamy gave a simple exposition of the gift of the Holy Spirit, based upon the Scriptures, added his own personal testimony, and then exhorted the people to receive the gift. The steps were simple: die to sin; receive the Holy Spirit; live unto righteousness.

Then the preacher urged each individual to mark out a spot just for himself, fall upon his knees in prayer, and *"tarry until"* he had received the assurance of the fulness of the Holy Spirit in his life. (Because of this emphasis of "tarrying until," these meetings came to be known in common parlance as "until meetings.")

By evening the landscape was dotted with individual seekers scattered all across the countryside, and the quiet of the evening was broken by a volume of petition ascending unto the Heavenly Father from scores of hungry hearts. Some of the workers walked up and down the hillside, giving special guidance and encouragement to those who needed counseling. No one was in a hurry; no one looked at the clock. All tarried until the Spirit came in refining power.

Then when the very last one had "prayed through," the entire group reassembled and joined in triumphant procession, marching up and down the hillside, singing and shouting the praises of God. Sometimes the procession lasted for two or three hours, breaking up in early hours of the morning. The group then partook of their feast of curry and rice and departed for their villages and homes. Then Veeraswamy went to another village.

When Dad returned from annual conference in Kolar he heard of this remarkable Spirit-led movement under the direction of Brother T. C. Veeraswamy. He got into his Model T. Ford and went out into the district to see the sight for himself. In village after village he witnessed these "until meetings." Dad was careful not to take over direction of the movement, but was content to sit by and watch God and His chosen leader carry the movement forward. For now he was seeing with his own eyes the answer to his most earnest prayer. This was Pentecost—in our day—in India—among the simple, village folk—in God's own way—and through Indian leadership! Truly God is no respector of persons or countries. Christ is "the same yesterday, and to day, and for ever." And the gift of the Holy Spirit is for all!

The results of this modern Pentecost abide to this day in the life and work of the Hyderabad and South India conferences. The original camp meeting of Bondla Bhavi has now developed into the famous Dharur Camp Meeting, which meets annually in a wooded area just outside the little town which bears the same name. This camp has been the spearhead of the evangelistic movement in that section of India for the past forty years. The annual attendance has increased to more than six-thousand, the majority of whom are simple village people who hear the message of Christ, are converted and filled with the Holy Spirit, and then go back to their homes and villages to witness to the transforming grace of the Lord Jesus Christ. As a result, in the past four decades the membership of the Church of Jesus Christ in that area has increased from seventy-five thousand to almost two hundred thousand, and even now each year a few thousand new converts are brought into the Kingdom and the Church.

Pentecost is more than just a historical fact; it is a present possibility. What happened more than nineteen hundred years ago can take place now in the twentieth century. What happened in Jerusalem on that day can happen today in Mount Vernon, Ohio, or Bondla Bhavi in India—anywhere that God's people tarry and pray and believe. What happened in the hearts of the disciples on the first Pentecost can take place in your heart in a personal Pentecost today! "TARRY UNTIL"!